Leonardo da Vinci

Georgia Clarke

Level 4

Series Editors: Andy Hopkins and Jocelyn Potter

Pearson Education Limited
Edinburgh Gate, Harlow,
Essex CM20 2JE, England
and Associated Companies throughout the world.

ISBN: 978-1-4479-6771-2

This edition first published by Pearson Education Ltd 2010

7 9 10 8

Text copyright © Georgia Clarke 2010

Illustrations by Sarah Horne c/o Advocate Art

The moral rights of the authors have been asserted in accordance
with the Copyright Designs and Patents Act 1988

Set in 11/13pt A. Garamond
Printed in China
SWTC/07

Published by Pearson Education Ltd

Acknowledgements
The publisher would like to thank the following for their kind permission to reproduce their photographs:
(Key: b-bottom; c-centre; l-left; r-right; t-top)
Alamy Images: Danita Delimont 70; **Biblioteca Comunale Cesenatico:** 59; **Bridgeman Art Library Ltd:**
British Museum, London 17; National Gallery of Art, Washington DC, USA 29; National Gallery, London
34; Royal Library, Windsor, Berkshire, UK 43; **Commune di Vinci:** 2; **Corbis:** Alinari Archives 60, 65;
Bettmann ivtr, 5, 12; Edimedia 30; Gianni Dagli Orti ivtc, ivtl; The Gallery Collection 44; **iStockphoto:**
Dan Prat ivbc; Jsemeniuk ivbr; M Evans ivbl; **RMN:** Rene-Gabriel Ojeda 15; Thierry le Mage 54, 55; **The
Royal Collection © 2009 Her Majesty Queen Elizabeth II**: 7, 19, 22, 25, 50, 67; Scala London: Photo
Scala, Florence - courtesy of the Ministero Beni e Att. Culturali 36; **Staatliche Museen Preussischer
Kulturbesitz**: Museum of Prints & Drawings 48; **© The Trustees of The British Museum**: 52
All other images © Pearson Education

Picture Research by Hilary Luckcock

For a complete list of the titles available in the Pearson English Active Readers series, visit www.pearsonenglishactivereaders.com.
Alternatively, write to your local Pearson Education office or to
Pearson English Readers Marketing Department, Pearson Education, Edinburgh Gate, Harlow, Essex CM20 2JE, England.

Contents

1.1 What's the book about?

How much do you already know about Leonardo da Vinci?

1 Where was Leonardo from?

    a Florence   **b** Venice   **c** Vinci

2 When was he born?

    a 15th century   **b** 17th century   **c** 19th century

3 Which of these paintings is by Leonardo?

  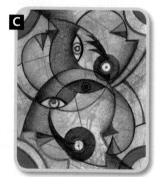

4 Which of these is it believed that Leonardo had the first idea for?

1.2 What happens first?

Look at the pictures in Chapter 1. Tick (✓) the towns that you think were important in Leonardo's life. Then discuss with other students why you think they were important.

London ☐   Paris ☐   Florence ☐   Madrid ☐

Vinci ☐   Rome ☐   Naples ☐   Milan ☐

Leonardo's Life and Times

Leonardo was, first of all, a painter and an artist. ...
But he was also a great thinker.

There are few people today who have never heard the name Leonardo da Vinci. But it is five hundred years since he died, in a small town in northern France. Why is his name still so well known? Who was he, and what did he give to the world?

Leonardo was, first of all, a painter and an artist who wanted to examine, describe and show through his work the beauty of the natural world. But he was also a great thinker. He hoped to use his understanding of nature to invent and build machines that would improve the world he lived in. Leonardo was admired in his own time as an artist and as an inventor. Today, people still think that his paintings are beautiful, although only a small number of them exist. We also admire the cleverness of his inventions, although we only know these from his writings and his drawings.

In 1994 Bill Gates, then head of Microsoft, bought a book of Leonardo's writings and drawings for $30.8 million. The book is thirty-six pages long and is filled with Leonardo's scientific notes from the years 1508 and 1509. It is the only book of Leonardo's writings owned by a private person in modern times.

Leonardo was born in 1452 and died in 1519. This was during the time that we now call the Renaissance. The word 'renaissance' is French and means 'rebirth'. Renaissance was first used to describe this time in history, and especially Italian history, in the nineteenth century. But the idea of the Renaissance began in the fifteenth and sixteenth centuries. At this time, people were looking back to and admiring the literature and art of Greece and Rome from 2,000 or 1,500 years before. In the fifteenth and sixteenth centuries, artists and writers wanted to copy what they thought was beautiful from that distant time. They also compared the art and books that they were producing with works from the past. Some even thought of it as a competition.

At the same time, a number of people were excited about questioning the world around them. The great thinkers did not want just to accept ideas and facts that were told to them. They wanted to find out for themselves what was and was not true. Leonardo belonged to this group of thinkers, and he was one of the most important. He was always looking at nature and thinking about ideas to help him understand the world better. Many artists and thinkers were interested in science as well as art, but Leonardo was unusual because he was interested in a large number of subjects and he studied them in great detail. He enjoyed the natural world and the wonderful things he saw in it, and he never missed an opportunity to learn. He led the way for others in his studies.

Vinci

● Childhood in Vinci

Leonardo was born on 15 April 1452. His mother was called Caterina and his father was a lawyer called Piero da Vinci. This surname means 'from Vinci', and Vinci is the name of the small country town in the west of Tuscany in Italy where Leonardo was born. We know the day and hour – Saturday at around 10.30 p.m. – because his grandfather wrote it down. His grandfather, who was also a lawyer, lived in Vinci, but Piero worked in the Tuscan capital, Florence. Leonardo's parents were not married, but Leonardo was part of his father's family from his birth.

Leonardo probably spent much of his childhood in Vinci and the countryside around it. You can see from the photograph of Vinci opposite that it is a small town on a hill. It is surrounded by green fields and trees and there are valleys and other low hills. It is certainly clear from Leonardo's drawings and from his writings that he knew and loved countryside, birds and animals. He tells us that his first memory was of a bird.

● Leonardo and his family

We do not really know much about Leonardo's relationship with his father, or with his mother, who lived somewhere near Vinci. Leonardo lived with his grandparents in Vinci while he was young, in a house with a large vegetable garden. In 1457 his grandfather, Antonio, recorded that he shared his house with his wife, his son (Leonardo's father), Piero's wife and Leonardo. Leonardo's uncle, Francesco, was twenty-two at the time and sometimes lived with them.

By 1469 Antonio had died and Leonardo, who was then seventeen, was living with his father and other family members in Florence. Leonardo's first **stepmother**, Albiera, had died and Leonardo's father was now married to Francesca, who was twenty. Uncle Francesco and his wife also lived with them. Francesco did not have any children of his own, so perhaps he thought of Leonardo almost as a son.

By the time Leonardo's father died in 1504, at the age of eighty, Leonardo had nine half-brothers and two half-sisters. Piero did not leave anything to Leonardo when he died, but Francesco left all his property to Leonardo. Piero's younger children were not pleased about this, so there was a legal argument between the brothers led by Giuliano, the eldest. But by late 1514 it seems the anger had gone because Leonardo met Giuliano in Rome and did his best to help him in a business matter. Giuliano's wife wrote to Giuliano from Florence and sent her best wishes to Leonardo, who she said was 'a most excellent and special man'.

stepmother /'stepmʌðə/ (n) the wife of your father, who is not your mother

Some important dates and events in Leonardo's life

15 April 1452	Leonardo is born in Vinci, a small country town. Lives there with his grandparents, father and family.
1469	He has moved to Florence. Living with his father and family and learning how to be an artist. Studying with the artist Andrea Verrocchio, who makes both paintings and **sculpture**.
1472	He becomes an independent painter in Florence, although sometimes still works on paintings with Verrocchio.
By 25 April 1483, to December 1499	He has moved to Milan. Working for the Sforza family, who govern the city. Paints pictures, makes sculpture, works as an engineer and **architect**, and plans decorations for plays and parties.
16 March 1485	He sees the sun completely covered with the earth's shadow. Very interested in understanding the movements of the sun, moon and stars.
2 April 1489	He draws the bones of a human head. Studying the human body as a scientist, which also helps him to be a better painter.
December 1499	He moves away from Milan soon after the Sforza lose control of the government to the French. Travels to Mantua for a short stay, where he is welcomed as an artist. Then goes to Venice, where he gives the government advice on controlling an important river.
By 24 April 1500, to summer 1506	He has returned to Florence. Lives there most of the time – working for the government on a big painting in an important public building and on **military** jobs.
summer and winter 1502	He is working for Cesare Borgia, the Pope's son, as a military engineer in central Italy. Travels around looking at the defence of different towns. Also makes notes on all sorts of things that interest him – like the way boats with sails are moved by the wind, or the musical sound of falling water.
June 1506 to September 1513	He returns to live in Milan. Works for the French government there as a painter, engineer and architect. Makes a few visits back to Florence.
December 1513 to summer 1516	He moves to Rome because the Pope's brother, Giuliano de' Medici, has asked him to come there to work for him.
autumn 1516	He goes to live in France to work for King François I in Amboise. Is much admired by the king and is called 'The King's Painter', which is a sign of his special position.
by 10 October 1517	He is living in a house at Clos Lucé, on the edge of Amboise, given to him by the French king.
2 May 1519	He dies at Clos Lucé, to the sadness of his assistant and friend, Francesco Melzi, who has been with him for years.

sculpture /ˈskʌlptʃə/ (n) a piece of art made – or *sculpted* – out of wood, stone, metal or other materials

architect /ˈɑːkɪtekt/ (n) a person who plans buildings; *architecture* is the art and science of building

military /ˈmɪlɪtəri/ (adj) used by, or connected with, soldiers and armies

● Learning an artist's skills

At some time in the 1460s – certainly before 1469 – Leonardo had moved to Florence. By 1472 he began training as an artist with the painter and sculptor Andrea del Verrocchio, and some time within the next four years he was living in Verrocchio's house. It was quite usual at this time for both pupils and skilled assistants to live in the house of their employer and to pay for their living costs – a kind of rent.

Verrocchio was one of the chief artists in Florence at that time and he had a number of other artists working for him. Leonardo learned all the skills of a painter, which included how to make paints. This was an important skill because these could not be bought in shops. Instead, painters had to make paints from careful mixing of rocks and earth with egg or with plant oils. Leonardo probably also learned about sculpture from Verrocchio and his assistants. Verrocchio was a famous sculptor of **bronze**. Leonardo was taught how to mix and heat metals, how to make the shapes of the sculpture, and then how to clean and shine it when it was cold.

Leonardo had strong ideas about how people should study to be painters. A student needed to study carefully, detail by detail. It was important too to study only with people who shared your desire to learn. If you could not find people like this, you should work alone. Sometimes it was actually good to work alone: you could give your full attention to your study instead of listening to friends talking. But it could also be useful to draw with other people, because you would want to work as hard as they did, and you could learn from their successes and their mistakes.

A good pupil, Leonardo believed, tried to be better than his teacher and should never lose an opportunity to think about art or to learn. He wrote:

I have found it very useful when in bed in the dark to remember the details of the things I have studied; it helps to make them stay in the memory.

A student could imagine **landscapes** or fights or people's faces and clothes in the marks on a wall or the different stones in a wall.

● Leonardo's pupils and assistants

When Leonardo started to work for himself, a number of people came to work for him. Some of them worked with him for a long time and travelled with him when he moved from one city to another to live. Others stayed a much shorter time.

---

bronze /brɒnz/ (n) a hard, brown coloured mix of metals that was used to make sculptures and guns
landscape /ˈlændskeɪp/ (n) countryside, or a picture showing a view of countryside

There were two people who came to Leonardo when they were boys, probably as pupils, and then spent many years working and living in his house. The first was Gian Giacomo Caprotti. He came to Leonardo in 1490, aged ten, from a small village near Milan. Leonardo recorded how much he paid for clothes and shoes for Giacomo in the first ten months, but mainly he listed Giacomo's bad behaviour and what and how he stole from Leonardo, Leonardo's friends and others. Around 1494 in one of his notes, Leonardo called him Salai, and this was the name that he always used for him after this.

Salai stayed with Leonardo for many years. In 1497 in Milan Leonardo recorded the cost of a very expensive coat for him, silver in colour with green edges. He gave Salai the money to buy it; but Salai could still behave badly because he stole the change! Salai probably learned to behave better because Leonardo sent him from Florence to Milan as his messenger on business matters, and also, later, a number of times from Rome to Milan. Salai stayed in service with Leonardo when he moved to France in 1516, and was paid 100 écus* a year by the French government. He was described by them as Leonardo's 'servant', but this amount of money was much much more than a house servant was paid, so they probably meant that Salai was an assistant to Leonardo. It is not certain, though, where he was when Leonardo died.

The second person was Giovanni Francesco Melzi, known as Francesco. He was Milanese and probably came to Leonardo aged thirteen or fourteen when Leonardo lived in Milan for the second time. Francesco had been to school but probably learned to paint with Leonardo. But, just as importantly, he helped him with writing things down. In France with Leonardo, Francesco was described as 'the Italian gentleman who is with Leonardo' and he was paid 400 écus a year by the French – four times as much as Salai. Francesco helped Leonardo in his studies and Leonardo valued him a lot, as we shall see later. Francesco's feelings about Leonardo are clear from the letter he wrote to Leonardo's eldest half-brother on Leonardo's death:

He was like the best father to me,
I cannot say how much pain his death gave me. As long as I live
I will always be sad.

● What was Leonardo like?

We have a number of documents about the life of Leonardo, as well as his own writings. In the late 1520s Paolo Giovio, who perhaps knew Leonardo in Milan or Rome, said that Leonardo was very polite, generous and spoke in a pleasant way; he was also very handsome. Another writer also said that Leonardo was

---

* écu: an old French coin of quite high value

very attractive and that he had beautiful long hair. He tells us that Leonardo normally wore a short rose-pink jacket, at a time when the fashion was for long jackets. In 1550 another writer, Giorgio Vasari, wrote that Leonardo was very strong and that he loved horses and riding.

Leonardo was unusual for the time because by 1516 he did not eat meat, although we do not know if this was true all his life. He was also left-handed and his writing almost always ran backwards. This means that his sentences are read from right to left instead of from left to right. You will notice this in some of the pictures in this book. You can read Leonardo's writing by holding it in front of a mirror and then reading it. If you do this, all the letters and words are perfectly formed. He wrote like this because it was the natural way for him to use his pen, but we do not know if he painted only with his left hand.

Perhaps Leonardo described his idea of a perfect life when he wrote:

The painter sits relaxed in front of his work. He holds a very light brush with soft colour on it. He is well dressed in clothes he likes. His house is clean and full of lovely pictures. He often listens to people playing music for him or reading to him from good books.

'Good books' suggests serious works, and a list of Leonardo's own books tells us that he did have many that were serious. But his idea of enjoyable reading also included popular adventures and humorous stories.

Drawing of Leonardo around 1508, perhaps by Francesco Melzi. This shows Leonardo when he was about fifty-six. He has long hair, which he had all his life, and a long beard and short moustache. Leonardo probably grew a beard only when he was older.

● Leonardo's life and travels

Florence

Although he was born in Vinci, Leonardo thought of himself as a Florentine; in documents he called himself 'Leonardo da Vinci, Florentine' or even just 'Leonardo Florentine'. He probably lived there for about twenty years of his life, at different times. Florence was famous in Italy and beyond for its artists, and it was the place where he learned his art.

Leonardo lived through times of peace and war in Italy. Florence was mostly peaceful while he lived there. The city, and a large area of Tuscany round it, was governed by a big group of rich businessmen. There was a strong interest in art, literature and learning in Florence and much of Italy at this time. Many rich men and women wanted to spend money on new paintings and sculpture for their houses and for the churches and other buildings where they went to religious services. Leonardo's first paintings were for men and women like these.

Milan

We do not know why Leonardo decided to leave Florence, but some time between autumn 1481 and spring 1483 he moved to Milan. Milan was a rich capital city in northern Italy, and one of the biggest cities in Europe – only Paris and London were larger. It was governed by the Sforza family. They wanted good architects, artists, musicians, historians and writers to work in their city because it showed their own importance and the importance of their state: the arts were almost as important as money and military power at that time. When a single family or person governed a city, there was the chance of big jobs because they could spend large sums of money as they wished.

The most powerful man in Milan was Ludovico Sforza, although he did not officially govern the city until 1495. Leonardo wrote about himself around 1483 in a letter to Ludovico:

> *In times of peace I believe I can give complete satisfaction, equal to any other man, in architecture in the planning of both public and private buildings, and in guiding water from one place to another. Also I can make sculpture in **marble**, bronze or **clay**, and in painting I can do everything that it is possible to do, as well as any other man.*

Ludovico and Milan therefore offered Leonardo exciting opportunities. He painted pictures and staged theatrical events. He began work on some big bronze sculptures. He gave his opinions on building and engineering problems. He **surveyed** land and he advised how to control rivers and water. In the 1490s he

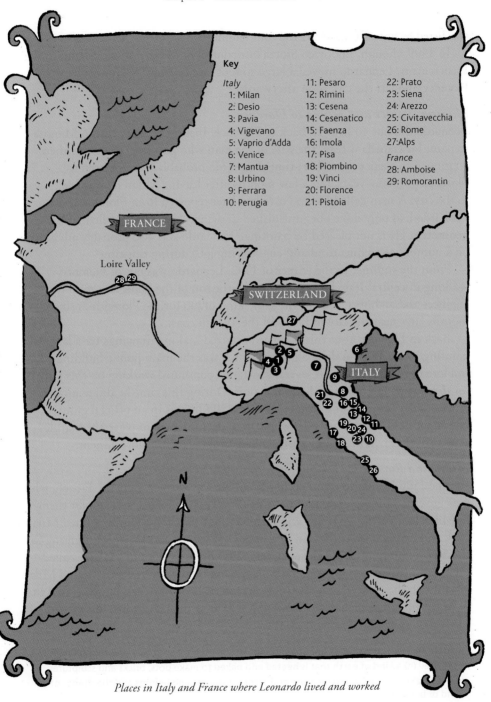

Key

Italy
1: Milan
2: Desio
3: Pavia
4: Vigevano
5: Vaprio d'Adda
6: Venice
7: Mantua
8: Urbino
9: Ferrara
10: Perugia
11: Pesaro
12: Rimini
13: Cesena
14: Cesenatico
15: Faenza
16: Imola
17: Pisa
18: Piombino
19: Vinci
20: Florence
21: Pistoia
22: Prato
23: Siena
24: Arezzo
25: Civitavecchia
26: Rome
27: Alps

France
28: Amboise
29: Romorantin

FRANCE

Loire Valley

SWITZERLAND

ITALY

N

Places in Italy and France where Leonardo lived and worked was listed as one of Ludovico's top four engineers.

In 1499, though, Ludovico Sforza lost control of Milan and all its land to the French army. Leonardo moved a large sum of money from Milan to a bank in Florence and left the city soon afterwards.

Mantua, Venice and return to Florence

Leonardo did not go straight back to Florence. Instead he went east to Mantua to paint for Isabella d'Este, the wife of the man who governed there. He then continued to Venice for a short time. Leonardo probably had not been to Florence for many years, but a few months after leaving Milan he was back in the city. A man called Pietro Novellara later reported from Florence that Leonardo had only done one, unfinished drawing; 'His mind is filled with **geometry**. He is not pleased by painting.' Leonardo was also probably advising on a number of architectural and engineering jobs during this time.

From the summer to the winter of 1502, Leonardo was out of Florence working in central Italy for Cesare Borgia, the son of the Pope, as a military engineer and architect. He did the same kind of job for the Florentines six months later near the city of Pisa and the Tuscan coast.

Back in Florence after this, Leonardo started making drawings for a large painting in the Palazzo della Signoria, which was the main public building in Florence. Leonardo, with several assistants, continued working on this job for three years but only finished some of it. During this time he did a number of other jobs as well. For example, in early 1504 he was in an official group of Florentines – mostly artists – who had to decide where to place the marble sculpture of David that Michelangelo had sculpted for the government.

Milan and Rome

In June 1506 Leonardo returned to Milan. He was welcomed by the French, who now governed the city. Leonardo was paid well by the French to work for them in Milan as an artist, engineer and architect. But the Sforza family wanted Milan back and Leonardo was there in December 1511 when Swiss soldiers, fighting for the Sforza family, attacked the area. Leonardo drew pictures of a village called Desio near Milan as it burned. There was more fighting in the area around Milan all through the next year. We are not sure where Leonardo was, but he stayed in or near Milan for much of the following year after the French had lost control of

---

marble /ˈmɑːbəl/ (n) a kind of smooth and shiny stone used for sculpture and for buildings
clay /kleɪ/ (n) a kind of earth that is heated and baked to make pots, bricks and sculptures
survey /səˈveɪ, ˈsɜːveɪ/ (v/n) to measure and record distances and heights and the shapes of land or buildings
geometry /dʒiˈɒmətri/ (n) the science of lines and shapes, like circles and squares

the city. In the autumn, though, Leonardo left Milan for Rome, where he lived for about three years as a guest of the Pope. Leonardo was sixty-one when he left Milan this time. He had spent about twenty-three years of his life there and it was a very important place to him.

France

But Leonardo had not been forgotten by the French. In the autumn of 1516 Leonardo accepted an invitation to go to France to the court of King François I in Amboise in the Loire Valley. Leonardo was much admired by François and was paid very well by him. He was given the title of 'The King's Painter'. The king also gave him a large house at Clos Lucé, on the edge of Amboise. In October 1517 it was reported that Leonardo had a weak right hand so he could not paint easily, but that he was still drawing and teaching.

Ten days before he died, Leonardo recorded what he would like to happen to his property after his death. He asked for his body to lie at the church of St Florentin in Amboise. Leonardo never married and there is no record that he had any children. He left all his books, painting equipment, **portraits**, his clothes and his money in France to Francesco Melzi. He gave a servant half of a garden on the edge of Milan, all the furniture from his house at Clos Lucé and money collected from boats using a **canal** in Milan. The other half of the Milanese garden Leonardo gave to Salai; Salai had already built a house there and Leonardo gave him that as well. He gave Maturina, a female servant, a good quality black coat with **fur** on the inside and two ducats*. To his brothers in Florence, Leonardo gave quite a large sum of money that was in a bank in Florence. From Melzi's letter we know they also got a farm at Fiesole, just north of Florence.

Leonardo died in his house at Clos Lucé on Monday, 2 May 1519.

* ducat: an old Italian coin with a high value

portrait /ˈpɔːtrət/ (n) a picture showing what a person looks like
canal /kəˈnæl/ (n) a man-made waterway for boats carrying people and other things
fur /fɜː/ (n) animal hair

2.1 Were you right?

Look at your answers to Activity 1.2 on page iv. Then complete these
sentences with the name of a town or city.

1 Leonardo was born in ....

2 He learned to paint and sculpt in ....

3 In .... he worked as an artist, engineer and architect for
the Sforza family.

4 He worked for the Pope in ....

5 He was known as 'The King's Painter' while he was living in the French
town of ....

2.2 What more did you learn?

By the end of Chapter 1 what do we know about Leonardo?

How would he answer these questions? Tick (✓) yes or no.

	yes	no
1 Have you got any full brothers or sisters?		
2 Do you paint pictures?		
3 Do you work with wood?		
4 Have you got short hair?		
5 Do you eat meat?		
6 Are you married?		
7 Have you got any children?		
8 Are you a sculptor?		
9 Do you know Michelangelo's work?		
10 Are you interested in nature?		

2.3 Language in use

**Look at the sentences on the right.
Then complete the sentences below,
using past perfect verb forms.**

> By 1469 Antonio **had died**.
>
> At some time in the 1460s
> Leonardo **had moved** to Florence.

1 Melzi worked for Leonardo after he ....*had left*............ (leave) school.

2 Leonardo's assistants lived in his house, as Leonardo .... (do)
  when he worked for Verrocchio.

3 By 1514, Leonardo's anger with his half-brothers .... (go).

4 Leonardo was one of the people who chose a place for the sculpture that

  Michelangelo .... (make).

5 By 1512, when Leonardo left Milan for Rome, the French .... (lose)
  control of the city.

6 By the time of his death, Leonardo .... (decide) who should have
  his property.

2.4 What's next?

**Read the title of Chapter 2, and the words in *italics* below it. What questions
do you think Leonardo asked himself to increase his understanding of how he
might paint the subjects below? Write some possible questions.**

1 landscapes

  How do colours change if there is more or less sunlight?.......................

  ....

2 people: their bodies, faces and clothes

  ....

  ....

3 animals

  ....

  ....

4 water

  ....

  ....

CHAPTER 2

Leonardo and Nature

'Nature has kindly given us things everywhere to copy', wrote Leonardo.
In all his activities, Leonardo was trying to discover the rules that control nature.

In the modern world, art and science are two very separate activities, but in Leonardo's time they were closely connected. Science meant mathematics and medical studies. How could these be connected with art? Mathematics included practical work like surveying land for making maps as well as measuring the movements of the stars in the sky. An artist might need to measure the different parts of the body. He could also use mathematics to place things in relationship to each other in a drawing or painting so the scene looked correct. You will see a good example in the painting of *The Last Supper* in the next chapter.

Mathematics was also connected to music because musical sounds have a fixed relationship with each other that can be described in numbers. Leonardo himself was a very good musician and liked to play an instrument and sing. More than this, though, Leonardo believed that numbers were a part of all things in the world and he said that 'without them nothing can be done.'

'Nature has kindly given us things everywhere to copy', wrote Leonardo. In all his activities, Leonardo was trying to discover the rules that control nature. In his search for those rules, he looked very carefully at a lot of examples and details. Actual experience was more important to him than opinion, and he worked from facts to ideas. Above all, Leonardo wanted to understand how and why things worked. His purpose was to examine the world so he could copy it in beautiful paintings and sculptures. But he also wanted to learn from the clever solutions of nature.

Leonardo was always drawing – quick little drawings to catch a movement or a shape, or more careful drawings done at a desk with a pen and ruler.

In July 2001 a small drawing by Leonardo was sold for $12 million. It was the most expensive drawing in the world.

● Light

Leonardo was a painter, and a painter needs to know about light and the effects of light. Your view of a hand or a rock or a tree is affected by the way light falls on them. Light and shadow help to bring them into view or make them disappear. Colour is affected by the brightness of light and the darkness of shadows. The effects of light also change at different times of day and even at different times of the year. Leonardo noted that the outside leaves of a tree take some blue from the colour of the air; the ones in the middle look more green because of all the other green leaves around them.

In his paintings, Leonardo wanted to copy the way that humans see light and colour, so his pictures would make you imagine real experience. When you look into the distance, for example from a hill out over the countryside, light affects how and what you see. Things get bluer but also less sharp if they are farther away from you. In the next chapter you can see this in some of the landscapes in his paintings.

Leonardo did not just look at things out in the world; he also positioned things so he could examine them in a controlled way. You can see this in the drawing below, where Leonardo is showing how light makes shadows as it comes through a window and falls on a ball. Leonardo drew and recorded studies like this carefully in a book.

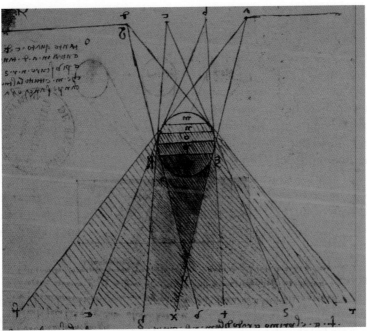

Light on a ball. The ball is seen from from above, with the window at the top of the page; the light from the window is shown as lines. Leonardo shows how the shadows fall behind the ball when light comes from slightly different directions through the window – as the sun moves during the day, for example. The shadow is always darkest where no light reaches it from the window.

Leonardo also looked at and thought about the sun, the moon and the stars. He discussed how light and heat come from the sun. He noted how the moon sends back light from the sun instead of having its own light. He talked about the size and measurements of the sun, moon and stars, and also how things can appear larger or smaller than they really are because of the effects of curves and distance. He did tests to prove these ideas; he did not just repeat what other people had said.

From his study of light, Leonardo wanted to understand sight. He examined human eyes, and even animals' eyes. Some animals and birds are awake at night and need to be able to see in the dark, and Leonardo noted that the centres of their eyes got larger when there was less light. He wrote that if you shone a light at a cat's eye in the dark, the eye looked like fire. We now know that this is because the back of a cat's eye is almost like a mirror. When light falls on it, it shines back. This helps the cat to see better at night. But Leonardo noticed that even a cat could not see if it was totally dark; then, he said, they used their excellent sense of smell to find their way around.

● Animals

There are all kinds of drawings by Leonardo of animals. Sometimes these are careful drawings with measurements of the different parts of an animal – a dog's head, a horse's leg. But opposite you can see an example of the way that he also tries to catch the character of an animal. In these quick drawings of a child with a cat we can see how interested he was in forms, movement and emotion. In the top drawing the child holds the cat with love and the cat pushes its head against the child. The cat's tail sticks up and its back legs move forwards as it climbs onto the child's legs. In the next drawing the child bends forward and runs his hand along the cat's back. You can almost hear the happy sound the cat makes. Then in the third picture the child holds the cat so tightly that the cat's body is bent out of shape. It looks less happy. Looking at these drawings you can imagine how the child and the cat feel, and they probably remind you of cats and children that you have seen yourself.

● Landscape, rocks, plants and trees

Leonardo filled pages and pages of paper with drawings and notes of the things that he saw and thought about. He wrote about types of rocks and how water moved, he recorded the plants that he saw growing in the countryside, and he studied the shapes of the land. For him the world was full of energy and natural forces; sometimes he even talked about the world as a living body.

When giving advice on painting, Leonardo told other painters:

You must leave your home in the town, and leave your family and friends, and go over the mountains and valleys into the country.

He also wrote that you needed to be alone to experience and study nature in

Drawings by Leonardo of a child and a cat

the fullest way. Leonardo tells us about some of his own experiences alone in the country and the effect they had on him. One day,

Pulled by my enthusiastic desire to see different and strange shapes made by nature, I walked some distance among dark rocks until I came to the entrance of a big hole in the side of a hill. I stood in front of this for some time shocked, not understanding it. Suddenly there were two emotions inside me: fear and desire. Fear of the heavy darkness and desire to see if there was anything wonderful inside the hill.

Emotions themselves interested him because as an artist Leonardo wanted to be able to understand how they affected people's faces and movements. He wanted to show feelings and thoughts in his paintings and sculpture.

Leonardo wanted to know about the smallest detail, and what was usual or unusual, so he wanted to see lots of examples of the same things as well as lots of different kinds of things. Leonardo showed many kinds of plants in his drawings and paintings, and his work is admired by scientists who study plants. When you look at the paintings in the next chapter, see how many different plants you can find and recognise.

● Water

Leonardo was very interested in water, from the smallest drops and streams to great rivers and seas. At least two of his books of notes are only about water. *The Codex Leicester*, as we call it now, which he wrote around 1507 to 1510, is all about the forms and power of water. In Milan from September to October 1508 Leonardo filled another book with notes under the title *Of the world and waters*.

Leonardo wanted to use these studies in two ways – first for his painting and second to control the movement of water and to make machines powered by water. He wanted to be able to paint not just rivers and seas but the way that water in the air changes the colour of the sky and affects how you see a distant view. He describes how he saw a storm on the River Arno:

The wind coming back hit the water and lifted it up, making a big hollow. The water was lifted straight up into the air. The colour was similar to that of a cloud. I saw this on the sand in the river. The sand was hollowed out deeper than the height of a man, and the sand and little stones were thrown around over a wide area. It appeared in the air like a really tall building and the top spread out like the branches of a really tall tree.

A number of Leonardo's later drawings show enormous storms. He wrote:

I have seen movements of air so angry that they have picked up the largest trees of the forests and whole roofs of big houses as they went. This same anger made a deep hollow and moved stones, sand and water a great distance through the air.

Drawings by Leonardo of the forms and movements of water. In the top two drawings, water meets different shaped things. The bottom drawing shows water falling from a height into a space. The water turns as well because it hits something at the edge.

These notes and drawings are reminders of the terrible power of nature to destroy. But for Leonardo there was also beauty in the forms and movements. His other drawings of water – like the one on page 19 – show this double character of water: great energy and very attractive and pleasing shapes.

The curves and movements of water were, said Leonardo, 'like hair'. He was also interested in making drawings of women's long hair, which was put up on their heads in complicated styles. These styles were very popular among young women in the fifteenth century. His interest in complicated curved forms also included drawings of knots. He used these ideas in interesting ways. He painted a room in the castle in Milan for Ludovico Sforza, and in it trees seemed to be growing up on all sides of the room. He painted the branches of the trees as the ceiling of the room, with all their green leaves. He wanted you to imagine that you were in a little wood in a garden. If you looked up through the branches, you could just see the blue sky above. Then a golden line of connected and complicated knots ran through and around the branches and leaves. So it seemed almost to be a garden building made of living wood.

● People

People were as much the subject of Leonardo's study as landscapes, animals and plants. To make a person in a painting or sculpture look real and alive, an artist needs to understand how a real body moves or how a living man or woman stands or sits. Artists, therefore, have to look very carefully at people. Their drawings record what they have seen. We have already seen an example of this in Leonardo's drawings of the child with a cat. Many of his other drawings are also of people and animals in movement.

He drew, for example, figures doing different activities. None of the figures wore clothes because he wanted to show clearly what happened to their arms, backs and legs as they worked. One drawing shows four men – or one man from different sides – who are digging. In another drawing, on the same sheet of paper, men are carrying packages and holding them in different positions. Drawings like these give a real sense of people's actions and activities.

If you were painting pictures of people, he said, you needed to know how they behaved – were they male, female, young, old? Were they rich or poor and what did they do? You needed to separate them into types and then separate them again so 'the men do not all appear to be brothers'. A friend of Leonardo in Milan wrote:

When Leonardo wanted to draw or paint a figure, he first thought about what kind of person they were. Then, when he had decided, he went to the places where he knew people of that kind could be found. He looked closely at their faces, their clothes, and the way they moved their bodies. He watched how they behaved. When he saw anything that he was looking for, he recorded it with a pencil in a little book which was always hanging from his belt.

Sometimes, it seems, Leonardo went one more step. When he wanted to draw laughing country men, we are told, he chose some and arranged a party for them. Then he told them stories until they laughed so much that they almost fell on the floor. He carefully watched their movements, and later made a drawing of them. This drawing had the same effect on people as his stories had.

Leonardo did not want to make his paintings of people so perfect that they were not real or they all looked the same: 'Beauty of the face may be equal in different people, but it never takes the same form,' he said. When you look at some of the paintings of young women in the next chapter, you can think about how Leonardo makes each of them different and recognisable. It is now very hard to see the details of his painting *The Last Supper*, but there too Leonardo wanted each of Christ's pupils to look different and to act differently from each other. This is because in his opinion every person feels emotion differently, and not everyone is going to have the same emotions either.

Leonardo also wanted to draw and paint correctly the clothes that people wore. As a young man he spent many hours practising drawing how real cloth fell around a body. He wanted to understand the forms and get the shadows right to make his art look real. Later he also wrote detailed descriptions of the forms of clothes and how they moved and lay differently as they fell over the body or over other clothes.

● Anatomy

Because doctors had to understand how all the parts of the human body worked, **anatomy** was also of interest to artists. In the fifteenth century, close examination of real bodies was only just beginning. Leonardo played a very important part in this study. In the beginning his drawings were of the way that bodies moved and the shapes and forms that were made when a body stood or sat, for example. Then Leonardo became more interested in examining the details of bodies and what lies under the skin.

In Florence, perhaps in 1507 or 1508, Leonardo was able to cut up some bodies of people who had just died. He said around this time that he had cut up more than ten bodies. This was hundreds of years before fridges were invented so bodies did not stay fresh for long. So when he wanted to understand all the **veins** of the body Leonardo had to cut up two bodies, one after the other, because it

anatomy /əˈnætəmi/ (n) the study of the inside parts, forms and connections of the human body

vein /veɪn/ (n) a part of the body like a tube through which blood moves

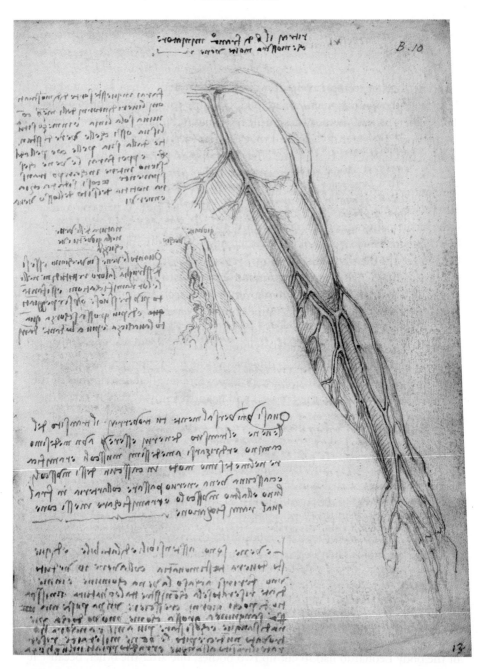

The veins in the arm of a man. In the little drawing Leonardo compares the veins of a boy with the veins of an old man – the boy's veins are straight and smooth and the old man's are curved and bent.

took some time to do his examination. He made drawings and detailed notes about what he saw.

One of the bodies was of an old man in Florence. Leonardo had met him just before he died:

> *This old man, a few hours before his death, told me that he had lived one hundred years and that he had no diseases but was just weak. And so, sitting on a bed in the hospital of Santa Maria Nuova, without any movement or sign of pain, he passed from this life. And I cut up his body to see what had made his death so kind.*

In the drawing opposite of a man's arm, we can see how Leonardo shows all the veins. Leonardo's study here centred on the movement of blood around the body, especially the veins. He compared the way blood moved through the body and the forms of veins with the movement of water and the shapes that streams and rivers make. He called the shapes of the veins in the body a 'tree'. So he was connecting his studies of the body with his studies of other parts of the natural world. To understand how the body worked, Leonardo was also interested in changes over time and the effects and signs of those changes. He was looking for reasons, not just at appearance or how things worked.

In spring 1510 Leonardo wrote that he believed he would finish all his work on anatomy. Perhaps he had a plan to produce a book on the subject. Leonardo thought, though, that his drawings showed things more clearly than words:

> *Oh writer, what words can you find to describe the whole arrangement as perfectly as in this drawing?*

But one drawing or view was not enough. To understand the body you needed to see it from different sides; for example, from the top, from below, and from each side of an arm or a leg. For the bone of an arm or leg you needed five views, because you had to cut through it. Often, though, Leonardo made even more drawings than this of a single body part.

◆

For Leonardo the natural world was always interesting and always full of rich ideas. The natural world was at the centre of his studies. In his opinion,

> *Although clever humans make different inventions, they can never find any inventions more beautiful, better matched to their purpose or clearer than nature's. In nature's inventions there is never too little or too much.*

To understand the natural world and to learn from it you had to keep studying. This was at the heart of Leonardo's art, his thinking and his inventions. But to understand the big picture, he said, you also had to study everything in the smallest detail.

3.1 Were you right?

Look at your answers to Activity 2.4. Then imagine that you are Leonardo and you are looking at the scene below. What details would you be interested in?

3.2 What more did you learn?

Are these sentences true (✓) or false (✗)?

1 There is no connection between music and mathematics.

2 Leonardo's drawings are not admired now.

3 Leonardo thought that colour was affected by light and shadow.

4 He believed that cats had a good sense of smell.

5 He was uninterested in people's thoughts and emotions.

6 Scientists today think that Leonardo drew plants badly.

7 Leonardo had the ability to tell funny stories.

8 People in Leonardo's paintings all look the same.

9 Artists in the Renaissance had little interest in medicine.

10 Leonardo was not interested in small details.

3 Language in use

Look at the sentence on the right.
Then report the sentences below in
the same way as the example.

> This old man, a few hours before
> his death, **told me that he had
> lived** one hundred years ...

1   Leaves on trees are different
colours because of their position
and the way light falls.

He said that leaves on trees were different
colours because of their position and the
way light fell .

2   The cat's shape will change
when it is picked up.

He explained that ....
....
....

3   I felt both fear and desire in front
of the hole in the hill.

He wrote that ....
....
....

4   Painters must leave their homes
and visit the country.

He believed that ....
....
....

5   I have cut up bodies to look at
the veins.

He told people that ....
....
....

3.4 What's next?

Look at the pictures in Chapter 3. Discuss the kinds of people that you think
Leonardo painted.

Leonardo the Painter

'You can see all sides of a sculpture, but painting has to give you the idea
of something round when really you are looking at a flat surface.'

L eonardo thought that a painter could tell a story more easily and
immediately than a writer by showing exactly how things looked. He also
compared painting with sculpture:

I myself have worked as much on sculpture as painting. Sculpture needs
light and shadow to look good but a painting has its own light and shadow.
Painting also uses and shows colour and distance in ways that sculpture
cannot. You can see all sides of a sculpture, but painting has to give you the
idea of something round when really you are looking at a flat **surface***.*

So he thought painting was better than sculpture and needed more skill. He also
thought it was important for a painter to show his work to others and to listen to
their opinions on it. He did not just mean other painters; everybody, he said, is
able to judge how natural things look and can see whether a painting looks right
or not.

● Leonardo's paintings

Leonardo was able to work as an independent painter in Florence from at least
1472, but he also continued to paint for Verrocchio and he was still living in
Verrocchio's house in 1476. Two years later, Leonardo was asked to paint a
religious picture for the Palazzo della Signoria in Florence. We do not know why,
but it is believed that he did not complete this painting, although he was given
some money for it. All through his life, Leonardo failed to finish paintings.

Leonardo never wanted just to copy what had been done in the past. For
example, he tried new methods and new ways of using paint in his paintings. It
was traditional in Italy to make paints with egg – this is called *tempera* in Italian.
These paints dried very quickly, which meant that you could not make changes
easily. But Leonardo, like other Italian artists, was interested in learning how to
make paint with oil instead of egg. This method had been invented by artists
in Northern Europe and was coming into fashion in Italy in the 1470s. It made
paintings much brighter because of the way light and colour shone through the
oil. Painters could build very thin coats of one or more colours to add to the
effects. The oil paint also dried more slowly, which meant that you could spend
a longer time working on getting a painting as you wanted it. In his portrait of
Ginevra de' Benci, Leonardo used a mix of oil and egg, so he was learning how to

surface /'sɜːfəs/ (n) the outside or top of something

use this new way of painting.

This picture, like all Leonardo's paintings that can be moved, was painted onto a wooden board. But the last paintings in this chapter – *The Last Supper* and *The Battle of Anghiari* – were painted onto walls. Artists used a different method for this kind of painting. It was important that the paint stuck to the wall, almost becoming part of the wall – this is called *fresco* in Italian. So you had to paint while the surface of the wall was slightly wet and this meant that you painted the picture a little at a time, day by day. But when the surface was dry, some artists then painted on top of what they had already painted, adding details or changing things.

Leonardo was one of these painters. But this paint did not stick to the wall in the same way as the paint on a wet surface, so these additions could disappear as time passed. This may be why *The Last Supper* is in such bad condition and lots of details have disappeared. Although it was painted in the middle of the 1490s, it was already damaged by 1517.

The Madonna of the Yarnwinder is a painting that many people think is by Leonardo. It shows the Virgin Mary with baby Jesus holding a stick onto which wool is placed. It was stolen from a Scottish castle in 2003, where it had been for over 200 years. It was found again by police in October 2007. The painting was valued at $65 million. This high value is because people think Leonardo is a great painter, and also because there are very few paintings by him.

● Portraits

Leonardo was very interested in painting pictures of real people, especially their faces. This was a type of painting that was becoming popular during the fifteenth century. It was a time before cameras were invented, so it was rare and special to have a portrait made. Sometimes it was because of a special occasion; for example, around the time of marriage of a young woman or man. But the rich could afford to have such paintings made because they wanted to – as a sign of their importance, or to record the face of someone they loved. Leonardo was famous for making portraits that people recognised. In 1503 one Florentine, Luca Ugolini, wrote to another, Niccolo Machiavelli, on the birth of Machiavelli's son: 'Congratulations! Your son looks just like you. Leonardo da Vinci could not do a better portrait.'

We have about five portraits by Leonardo; four of them are of young, rich women. We can name nearly all of the women shown and in some cases we know why their portraits were painted and who they were painted for. In other cases we have to do some detective work to try to discover their secrets, although there are still unanswered questions.

One of Leonardo's earliest portraits, of Ginevra de' Benci, was painted in Florence when Leonardo was in his twenties. In the landscape in the background, we can see Leonardo putting into practice his wish to give you the sense of looking far out over countryside. The browns and greens disappear into the distance and become blue, which meets the light from the sky. These distant parts of the landscape are painted in a method called, in Italian, *sfumato*. This is an effect almost like looking through smoke, where colours and lines disappear into each other.

Leonardo gives us help in guessing who the subject of the portrait is. The name Ginevra is very close to the Italian word *ginepro*, which means **juniper**, and we can see lots of this plant behind Ginevra's head. So Leonardo was making a play on words in the painting. Ginevra was a Florentine and the daughter of a very rich man. Some people think that Leonardo painted this portrait in 1474 when, aged sixteen or seventeen, she married an important man in government. Ginevra looks at us out of the painting and in the fifteenth century this kind of behaviour suited a wife more than an unmarried girl. But Ginevra was not a woman who lived a completely private and hidden life; a number of men wrote poems about her. They wrote about what a good and intelligent person she was and said how beautiful her golden hair and brown eyes were.

It has been argued, though, that in the painting Ginevra looks older than seventeen. On the back there are also some signs that Leonardo painted it not for Ginevra's husband or for her or her family, but for an admirer. Leonardo painted a branch of juniper between branches of two other plants; the branches are connected by painted words which say 'beauty decorates goodness'. The plants also had **symbolic** meanings. So Leonardo used both pictures and words to tell us that Ginevra was beautiful, good and pure. He was also perhaps showing that she loved somebody or that somebody loved her.

It was common for men, who lived in a hard world of war and business, to talk about love for a special woman as a way to show their gentler emotions, often in the artistic form of poems or songs. The woman was often not their wife, but it did not always mean that there was any hope of such love being physical and sexual.

---

juniper /'dʒuːnɪpə/ (n) a plant with sharp leaves and a strong smell
symbolic /sɪm'bɒlɪk/ (adj) using one thing or picture to mean another; for example, a flag is a *symbol* of a country

Ginevra de' Benci, *National Gallery of Art, Washington, D.C., USA.*
When Leonardo was painting this picture, in the mid-1470s, he wanted to mix colours together and soften some lines. Instead of doing this only with a brush, he sometimes used his fingers – he left the marks of his fingerprints in places. The plant behind Ginevra was bright green, but the paint has got browner with age. The lower part of the painting was cut off later, so we cannot see Ginevra's hands now. This is the only one of Leonardo's portraits in the Americas.

● The Lady with an Ermine

The Lady with an Ermine, *Czartoryski Collection, Krakow, Poland.*
Leonardo probably painted this around 1489 or 1490.

Not all love was non-physical or found only in marriage. We can see this in Leonardo's painting of *The Lady with an Ermine.* This painting shows Cecilia Gallerani, who was the lover of Ludovico Sforza, the most powerful man in Milan. Leonardo painted this picture in Milan, perhaps for Ludovico or maybe for Cecilia herself, because she owned the painting by 1498.

Leonardo had been in Milan at the Sforza court for six or seven years when he painted this portrait. Perhaps he already knew Cecilia, but his skill in this portrait was to bring her to life for us. She turns to her left. Has she heard or seen someone or something? Her position is natural and her rich clothes also have natural forms. This sense of life in a painting was something that Leonardo thought was really important. Around this time he wrote that a good painting of a person is one where 'the behaviour of the person in the picture shows the energy that is inside them.'

In 1492 Bernardo Bellincioni wrote a poem about Leonardo's portrait of Cecilia in which he **praised** the painting for those same qualities. He tells nature not to feel that she has lost a competition with Leonardo as Cecilia's portrait is so good; nature, of course, made both Leonardo and Cecilia.

praise /preɪz/ (v/n) to say what is really good about something or somebody, or what is very well done

Bellincioni's 1492 poem

Oh Nature, what has annoyed you? Who are you jealous of?
Of Vinci, who has painted a portrait of one of your stars,
Cecilia, who is so beautiful today that
in comparison with her beautiful eyes the sun seems a dark shadow?

The praise is for you if in his painting
he makes her seem to listen, and almost speak.
Think how you will get more praise in the future
if she looks more alive and beautiful.

Therefore now you can thank Ludovico
and the skill and hand of Leonardo
who wish to give her to the future.

Whoever sees her like this, even too late
to see her alive, will say this is enough
now for us to understand both nature and art.

The animal in Cecilia's arms is an **ermine**. Leonardo wrote that the ermine: *prefers to let itself be caught by hunters instead of entering a dirty place to save itself. This is because it does not want to mark its pure nature.*

The whiteness of the ermine's fur is symbolic of purity, so the ermine here shows that Cecilia had a clean and perfect character. But Leonardo had not finished playing games with words. The Greek for ermine was *galé*, so he was making a clever joke on Cecilia's surname – Gallerani. The ermine also reminds us of Cecilia's lover, Ludovico, who was made a member of an organisation called the Order of the Ermine in 1488 by the king of Naples. It had only twenty-seven members, who were heads of governments or top soldiers.

Cecilia's portrait by Leonardo was famous and in April 1498 Isabella d'Este, the sister of Ludovico Sforza's wife Beatrice, wrote to Cecilia to ask her if she would lend it to her. Isabella had just seen some beautiful portraits by the Venetian painter Giovanni Bellini, and wanted to compare his work with Leonardo's.

Cecilia sent the painting immediately. She wrote, though, that she would be happier to send the painting if it looked more like her:

---

ermine /ˈɜːmɪn/ (n) a small animal that lives in the countryside. Its special quality is that in the summer its fur is reddish-brown and in the winter it turns white but its tail stays black.

*But this is not because of any fault in the great painter himself – I truly
believe there is no painter equal to him – but only because the portrait was
painted when I was very young. I have changed completely since then.*

The letters, and Bellincioni's poem of 1492, show us how famous Leonardo
was as a painter and how people wanted to see his works.

● The Mona Lisa

Leonardo's *Mona Lisa* or *La Gioconda* is perhaps the most famous painting in the
world today. The painting, though, contains many mysteries. We are not certain
who the portrait is of, and maybe it was not a real woman. The name Mona
Lisa appeared first in 1550, when Giorgio Vasari wrote about Leonardo's life in a
book describing the lives and works of Italian artists. Vasari said that in Florence
Leonardo started a portrait of Lisa Gherardini, who was the wife of Francesco
del Giocondo. Mona is a short way of saying Madonna – 'my woman', which in
Italian was a polite title for a wife – so Mona Lisa means Mrs Lisa. The other
name for the painting, *La Gioconda*, can be understood in two ways: Mrs del
Giocondo, or the 'happy' or 'playful woman'.

We are not sure when Leonardo painted the portrait, but it was probably
when he was in Florence between 1503 and 1506. Lisa was born in 1479 and
married the rich businessman Francesco in 1495, so she was about twenty-four
to twenty-seven when Leonardo was in Florence. The colour of the painting now
is rather yellow. This was not what Leonardo intended – Lisa's skin should be
paler and whiter, more like the skin of Ginevra de' Benci or Cecilia Gallerani.
Light and dirt have affected the painting and made it look darker.

Leonardo painted the woman sitting on a chair. She is in front of a window
or an opening to the landscape beyond. In the distance water and sky meet, but
on the left we can see a clear path through rocky hills to the lake or river, and
on the right-hand side there is a bridge across a valley. So Leonardo is telling us
with these signs of man's presence that this landscape is not completely empty; it
has been made and is lived in by people. It reminds us of Leonardo's interest in
natural forms as well as useful human inventions.

The woman sits calmly with her hands crossed. She is separate from the
landscape, but the softness and darkness of her hair and clothes connect her
with it. This is a famous example of Leonardo's use of *sfumato* and the way that
it gives a feeling of mystery for us looking at the picture. But Leonardo also
included clear details, like the decoration at the top of her dress. She seems to
look straight at us – Leonardo wanted to make people think that in a portrait
they were looking at a living person.

Is Mona Lisa smiling? If she is, what is she smiling at? What does her smile mean? These are questions that almost every visitor to the Mona Lisa in the Louvre asks. Is the smile just a play on her name? Or was Leonardo trying to show an imaginary woman whose smile symbolised the peace inside her?

Mona Lisa, *Louvre, Paris, France*
This painting has belonged to the French government from soon after Leonardo's death. On 21 August 1911 the picture was stolen, but it was found again in 1913. Since then it has only left the Louvre in Paris twice. This painting is so famous that it is protected from attack by thick glass. On some days thousands of people come to see it; even more since the book and film The Da Vinci Code.

● Religious paintings

Leonardo began a number of religious paintings that people asked him to make for churches. He did not always manage to complete them. Sometimes we know about such paintings partly or totally from drawings that he made when he was preparing them.

The Virgin of the Rocks

The Virgin of the Rocks is a picture that Leonardo painted twice. One painting is in the Louvre in Paris, France, and the other is in the National Gallery in London, England. For a long time it was believed that the London painting was by another painter and not by Leonardo himself, but many people now believe that the London painting is by Leonardo. But why did Leonardo paint this picture again, almost exactly the same? In 1483, probably very soon after he had arrived in Milan from Florence, Leonardo agreed to paint a picture of the baby Christ with his mother (the Virgin Mary) a baby St John the Baptist and an **angel** for the church of San Francesco. The painting was perhaps completed by 1485. But this was not the end of the story. We do not know if it did not please the people who had asked for it, or if there was a problem about money – possibly both. There are legal documents from the early 1490s in which Leonardo said he had not received enough money for the painting, and that someone else wanted to buy the painting

The Virgin of the Rocks, *National Gallery, London, England*

angel /ˈeɪndʒəl/ (n) a messenger of God

for more. Leonardo did sell it, we believe – perhaps to this person. This is the painting in the Louvre. Then, sometime between 1491 and 1508, Leonardo painted the second one for the church. This is the one in the National Gallery.

The Virgin of the Rocks shows how Leonardo used his interest in plants and rock forms to give us a sense of the Virgin, Christ, St John and the angel in the natural world, with mountains and water in the background. Leonardo painted the plants carefully, so you can see the leaves and flowers of the different kinds of plants. He did this partly because of the symbolic meanings of these plants; for example, the white flowers in the front on the left remind us of the purity of the Virgin. The wings of the angel look like the wings of a bird, and therefore help to make us think that the angel really can fly. Leonardo brought together the real, symbolic and imaginary worlds to make the picture believable; this was his skill.

We know that people in the sixteenth century admired both paintings of *The Virgin of the Rocks* because at least twelve copies were made by other artists of the first picture and there were also twelve copies made of the second one.

The Last Supper, Monastery of Santa Maria delle Grazie, Milan, Italy

In 1494 or 1495, Leonardo was asked by Ludovico Sforza to paint one of his most famous pictures. Ludovico wanted him to finish it quickly and it was probably completed in February 1498. But, as usual, Leonardo did not paint fast. Matteo Bandello was a young man at **Monastery** of Santa Maria delle Grazie when Leonardo was painting. Later he wrote:

Leonardo arrived early, climbed up to the picture and started to work Sometimes he stayed there from sunrise to sunset, never putting his brush down, forgetting to eat or drink. Other times he spent two, three or four days without touching a brush, but each day he spent several hours in front of the work looking, examining and criticising the figures to himself. I also saw him, as the wish or desire took him, leave another job at midday – when the sun is highest – and come to Santa Maria delle Grazie. Climbing up to the picture, he took a brush, added a little to one of the figures, then immediately left.

In fact Leonardo did not work alone on the painting as this suggests; pupils and assistants helped.

This painting is *The Last Supper*, which shows Christ eating with his pupils the night before his death. It was painted on one complete wall of the real dining-room of the monastery: as the **monks** ate their food, they could see and be reminded of Christ and his pupils as models for their own life and behaviour.

---

monastery /ˈmɒnəstri/ (n) a large building lived in by a group of very religious Christian men
monk /mʌŋk/ (n) a member of an all-male religious group that lives separately from other people

Leonardo wanted the monks to imagine the thoughts of each of the men sitting at the table: Christ has just told these men that one of them will do him harm. Only one of the thirteen pupils – Judas Iscariot – knows who that person is. The others wonder, and some are afraid that it might be them. Leonardo has tried to show us this situation by making each of the figures look and act differently. Leonardo wrote around this time that 'the movements of men are different because of the thoughts in their minds.'

The Last Supper, *Cenacolo of Santa Maria delle Grazie, Milan, Italy*

The Last Supper was repaired between 1977 and 1999. The repairs cost over $9 million. Only 400 people a day are allowed to see the painting. They can visit in groups of not more than twenty-five for just fifteen minutes. This is to control the quality of the air in the room.

Leonardo used his mathematical abilities to make it seem that the dining-room continues. He wanted to place everything in relationship to each other so it would look correct to us. This is very clear from the strong lines of the ceiling, windows and doors of the room where the supper takes place. Leonardo wanted us to imagine that the event was happening in front of our eyes. Christ sits, almost alone, in the centre of the painting and the table. Behind his head and to each side we can see a distant landscape through the open windows, so we see Christ not only in relationship to the men around him but also to the natural world beyond.

● A competition with Michelangelo?

Leonardo had become famous in Milan, but he was also famous in his home city, Florence. There, in 1503 he was asked to paint a very large painting on a wall in one of the main public rooms of the Palazzo della Signoria. *The Battle of Anghiari* would show a great fight which the Florentines had won against Milan in 1440. It was an important point in Florentine history.

Leonardo finished a part of the drawing for the painting in 1505. It was taken to the Palazzo della Signoria and used to mark on the wall where the figures of the horses and men would be placed. Leonardo then began work on painting the picture on the wall. At the same time, Michelangelo Buonarroti was asked to paint another scene from Florentine history in the same room in the palace. Michelangelo was a younger Florentine sculptor and painter who was also much admired at this time. So the Florentine government had chosen two of its greatest living artists to celebrate its history with two important military and political wins against enemy states. Leonardo and Michelangelo probably did not work in the same room at the same time, but it was impossible not to see the work of the two artists as a competition.

You will perhaps not be surprised to know that Leonardo had not finished his painting when he left Florence in June 1506 to go back to Milan. Michelangelo had left Florence a year earlier to go to Rome to work for the Pope. He later returned to Florence for a short time, but he never did more than parts of his very large drawing. But although neither work was finished, other painters came to study and copy them. Michelangelo's drawing was destroyed in 1516, but Leonardo's painting could be seen until the 1550s.

4.1 Were you right?

Think back to your answers to Activity 3.4. Then circle below words which describe the kinds of subjects that Leonardo painted.

religious scenes   rich, important people   animals

ships   war scenes   towns   landscapes

his family   beautiful women   machines

4.2 What more did you learn?

Which painting does each of the following describe?

1 This painting shows an important fight between the Florentines and the Milanese that took place in 1440. It was paid for by the Florentine government. Leonardo painted the heat of the battle with soldiers on horses right up against each other, so you can imagine the noise and the bravery and also the fear on both sides.

2 In this painting Leonardo shows a beautiful young Milanese woman carefully holding a large white ermine. She is wearing an expensive blue and red dress with black decoration. Her right hand is very clearly pressing against the ermine's fur. This, and its size, suggest that the ermine is an important part of the painting.

A *Ginevra de' Benci*
B *Cecilia Gallerani*
C *Mona Lisa*
D *The Virgin of the Rocks*
E *The Last Supper*
F *The Battle of Anghiari*

3 Leonardo's interest in landscape and the natural world is clearly shown in this painting. The beautiful woman in the centre, dressed in blue and gold, shows you the two young children below. The child on the left holds a cross to symbolise that he is John the Baptist; he holds his hands together towards the other child. The other child is supported by an angel behind him. We know that he is Christ by the way he lifts his hand.

.3 Language in use

Look at the sentences in the box, then write *so*, *such* or *such a* in the spaces below.

> This may be why *The Last Supper* is in **such** bad condition.
>
> This painting is **so** famous that it is protected from attack by thick glass.

Why do people think that *Mona Lisa* is ¹............................... great painting? Is it because she is ²............................... beautiful woman? Or is it because she is ³............................... calm, or her smile is .... mysterious?

⁵............................... bright light falls on her face, and the areas around the face are ⁶............................... dark, that we cannot stop looking at it. But the landscape behind her shows ⁷............................... close connections between the human and the natural worlds that the painting is not a simple portrait. People visit the painting from around the world because it is ⁸............................... famous. It is also very, very valuable.

.4 What's next?

Read the first few lines of Chapter 4. Leonardo worked for just a few rich and powerful people. He also left his home town to do this. Discuss why you think Leonardo chose this kind of life, and make notes.

Notes

An Artist at Court

*'I see that rightly he is already famous for painting, but he has not
been praised enough for his many other very great abilities.'*

From 1483 until his death, Leonardo worked for a number of very powerful
men and women in Italy and France. Leonardo made things that pleased his
employers and many people admired his work. Some of them were also happy to
support his studies. In this chapter we will look at some of the things that he did
and some of the relationships that he had with his rich employers over the years.

Leonardo lived in Milan for sixteen or seventeen years, working at the Sforza
court, and then, after a few years in Florence, he moved back to Milan for about
four or five years and worked for the French government there. Then he was
in Rome for three years, where the Pope's brother gave him a place to live and
money for himself and his assistants. Finally, Leonardo moved to the royal court
of François I in France.

● Leonardo at work in Milan

In Milan Leonardo had the opportunity to work on a number of special
theatrical events. Plays were performed privately, and only for the richest and
most important people in a city. There were no theatres at this time, so a large
room in a big house was turned into a theatre for a day. This kind of event
usually happened to celebrate a wedding or sometimes if a really important
person, like a king or the head of government of another state, came to visit.
The hosts wanted to show that the city and state was rich and that its artists and
writers were skilled. This is another reminder of how much art and literature
were valued at this time.

Leonardo planned the stage for a play that took place on 13 January 1490
to celebrate the marriage of the daughter of the king of Naples to the man who
governed Milan. The play was specially written by Bernardo Bellincioni and it
was called *Il Paradiso*, which means 'Heaven'. Leonardo made 'heaven' in the
form of half of a big egg covered with gold on the inside and with lots of lights as
stars. At the top were twelve pictures of groups of stars – one for each month of a
year – lit with flames behind glass. Around 'heaven', seven men moved in a circle
– probably on some kind of hidden moving platform. Each man was dressed in
wonderful clothes to look like a god who governed each of the seven main stars –
the sun, the moon, Mercury, Venus, Mars, Jupiter and Saturn. Leonardo made a
'heaven' again a few years later for another play, *Danaë*, with 'Jove and the other

gods lit by a great number of lamps like stars.' All this took place to the sound of music. Many of the figures in the play appeared from above and hung in the air to make their speeches or to sing.

Leonardo worked on a different kind of event for a double celebration in January 1491, when Ludovico Sforza married Beatrice d'Este, a daughter of the man who governed Ferrara. Ludovico was thirty-nine and Beatrice was sixteen and it was a political marriage. At the same time her brother married Ludovico's niece. Leonardo's job was to plan the clothes and the theatrical part of a formal military event. In this event two men on horses rode towards each other fast, each holding a long, sharp piece of wood. The purpose was to knock the other person off their horse. Riders fought a number of times against different people. They needed great skill and bravery as they could easily get very badly hurt or die. The riders were dressed in beautiful clothes and the horses were covered in expensive cloths.

● The Sforza horse

One of Leonardo's biggest jobs while he was in Milan was to make an enormous bronze sculpture of Ludovico Sforza's father, Francesco Sforza. Francesco had been a great soldier and had taken control of Milan in 1450. He died in 1466. The sculpture would show Francesco dressed as a soldier on a horse. The Sforza family had wanted to find someone to make this sculpture for years. Leonardo knew this and when he wrote to Ludovico in 1483 he finished the letter: 'It will be possible to make the bronze horse.'

For this job Leonardo was able to bring together his love of horses and the sculptural skills he had learned from Verrocchio. We know that he was drawing horses in Milan. He made notes about horses that belonged to members of the Milanese court:

Mariolo's shiny black Florentine horse is a big horse. It has a beautiful neck and quite a beautiful head. The white male horse of the man responsible for the hunting of birds has beautiful back legs.

There are drawings by Leonardo of horses moving and standing, and of details of legs and chests and heads, as well as measurements of all their different parts. One writer has suggested that for the sculpture Leonardo wanted to put together the most beautiful parts of the most attractive horses to make the perfect horse! Leonardo was also looking at Roman and more recent big bronze sculptures of horses for ideas. In the fifteenth century this kind of sculpture was new and difficult to make.

Leonardo was given rooms in an enormous old house belonging to the Sforza

Drawings by Leonardo for the Trivulzio sculpture

family. It was called the Corte Vecchia and was in the centre of Milan near the main church. This was perhaps so he had enough space to make the horse, and room for the assistants that he needed as well. The horse was about eight metres tall and needed about 67,800 kilograms of bronze. Leonardo probably started this job in the middle of 1489, but it took years for him just to make the full size model out of clay. This was much admired by those who saw it. People said the horse looked alive. It was used as part of the decorations in the main church for the wedding of Ludovico's niece in 1493.

But Leonardo was out of luck. In 1494 the French army entered northern Italy on their way to fight for the city of Naples and to take control of all the south of the country. Ludovico was on the French side so Milan was safe, but soon he feared that the French might try to take Milan from him. He helped other cities that were fighting the French. One of the most important of these was Ferrara, where the head of the government was his wife's father. All the bronze for Leonardo's horse was sent to Ferrara to make big guns to use against the French. Leonardo wrote: 'Of the horse I will say nothing, because I know the times.' Then when the French did take control of Milan at the end of 1499, their soldiers destroyed the big clay model of the horse by shooting at it. It was, no doubt, heart-breaking for Leonardo.

But, around 1508, Leonardo had another chance to try to make a big bronze sculpture of a horse and rider, this time of a rich and powerful Milanese soldier – Gian Giacomo Trivulzio. Leonardo made a few drawings of ideas for it, like the one opposite, and we also have a list by him of how much it would cost. The total was 3,046 ducats. So you can see how expensive it was to make a sculpture like this and that it needed a lot of time and careful work. Leonardo had planned everything, but it was another of his plans that did not get beyond the first stages.

● Isabella d'Este and Leonardo

When Leonardo left Milan in the winter of 1499, he did not return to Florence but took the opportunity to go to the court in Mantua. Here Isabella d'Este was already, at the age of twenty-five, trying to get musicians, writers and artists to write and make things for her. Leonardo had perhaps already met her in Milan when she had come for the wedding of her sister, Beatrice, to Ludovico Sforza and on another, later visit. She certainly knew about Leonardo's art. We know how much she wanted to see a painting by Leonardo from the letter she wrote to Cecilia Gallerani about borrowing her portrait.

A drawing by Leonardo of Isabella d'Este

Isabella d'Este was very important. She was a daughter of Ercole d'Este, who governed Ferrara, and Eleonora, daughter of the king of Naples. At sixteen she married Francesco Gonzaga, who governed Mantua. She had money, power, and a great interest in art and literature. Famous for her strong character, she also used her political abilities to help both Mantua and her sons.

In Mantua Leonardo made two portrait drawings of Isabella, but she was never able to get a finished portrait painting from him. Another painter saw one of these drawings in Venice, and wrote to Isabella:

Leonardo da Vinci showed me a portrait of you which is very life-like. It is so well done that it is not possible to do better.

It seems that only one drawing still exists. You can see it opposite.

In March 1501, Isabella asked Leonardo to paint her a picture, because she wanted the best Italian painters to paint pictures for her. She said that if Leonardo did not want to do the one she wanted, maybe he would paint a little picture of the Virgin Mary. Her messenger had difficulty meeting Leonardo, and finally he asked Leonardo's assistant Salai to arrange it. Leonardo was careful to say how willing he was to please Isabella and how grateful he had been for her kindness when he was in Mantua. But he said that he did not want to paint and was working on geometrical studies. Also he had a painting to do for a Frenchman, connected to the French king, although he said he would prefer to do a painting for Isabella.

Isabella did not give up. In July 1501 she sent a letter to Leonardo by a different messenger, Manfredo de' Manfredi. Manfredi wrote to Isabella that he had put the letter into Leonardo's own hand and told Leonardo that he would send the reply for him. Leonardo did nothing, so Manfredi sent a servant to find out what had happened. Leonardo said that he could not write, but that he had begun doing what Isabella wanted. So, once again, Leonardo appeared to be willing to work for her but actually did nothing. Isabella did not get angry, because the following year she described him in a letter as 'my friend'. She asked Leonardo to look at some very old pots that were for sale in Florence. Isabella was an enthusiastic collector and wanted to make sure she got the best pieces at a good price. She was sent Leonardo's detailed opinion on each thing and why it was beautiful or special.

In May 1504 Isabella was still thinking of the portrait she had not received. She wrote to Leonardo in Florence that:

I am hopeful that I can get from you what I have so much wanted, which is to have something painted by you. ... When you were here and drew my portrait, you promised that sometime you would do one in colour for me. As this is now almost impossible, since it is not convenient for you to travel here, I hope that you will want to complete our agreement by turning it into a picture of the young Christ.

She had no luck with that idea either!

● Leonardo and the French in Milan

In May 1506 Leonardo asked the Florentine government to let him leave Florence for Milan. He had to get permission because he was still supposed to be working on the great painting of *The Battle of Anghiari* for them. They were not happy, but they agreed that he could go for three months. If he did not come back he would have to pay 150 florins* to the government. Leonardo needed to go to Milan because of the legal problems about the painting of *The Virgin of the Rocks*.

Milan was now under the control of the French king Louis XII. The thirty-three-year-old governor there was the Frenchman Charles d'Amboise. He was very happy to please Leonardo and to keep him in Milan. He gave Leonardo rooms in the Sforza Castle on the edge of Milan, in which he lived too. In early October the Florentine government wrote to Charles: 'Leonardo has not behaved correctly towards Florence because he has taken a large sum of money and done little for it.' They said that Leonardo must return to Florence and finish his work.

Charles did not reply for two months. When he did, he said that he would not stop Leonardo leaving Milan. But in his letter he said how wonderful he thought Leonardo was:

The famous works that Leonardo da Vinci, your citizen, has done in Italy, many in Milan, have made everyone love him even if they have not met him. I was among those who loved him before I knew him. Now that I have spent time with him, I can speak from experience of his abilities. I see that rightly he is already famous for painting, but he has not been praised enough for his many other very great abilities. ... I will be very grateful for everything that you can do either to increase his property or to reward him.

In this clever way he was saying how great he thought Leonardo was, but at the same time criticising the Florentines' rude and angry letter.

It seems that Leonardo did not really want to go back to Florence. He was in luck. In the middle of December a French official, working in Florence for King Louis, wrote to the Florentine government. He said that the king had seen one of Leonardo's pictures, which pleased him, and so the king wanted Leonardo to stay in Milan and paint something for him. There was also a formal letter from the king to Florence which was polite but made the situation quite clear:

I need Leonardo da Vinci, Florentine painter. Please write to him and tell him not to leave Milan before I arrive there.

The Florentine government had to agree.

Within three months of the king's arrival in Milan he was calling Leonardo

---

* florin: an old Florentine coin with quite a high value

'my painter and official engineer'; this was a sign of Leonardo's importance. More than this, though, he called him 'my dear and well loved Leonardo da Vinci'. During August 1507 it was said that Leonardo was working on 'a painting that is very dear to the king'. This praise from both Charles and King Louis XII shows that they admired Leonardo's abilities and skills as a painter, engineer and architect, but they also liked him very much as a person. Charles died in March 1511. He had done much to support Leonardo.

● Leonardo in Rome, 1513–16

'I left Milan for Rome on 24 September 1513,' wrote the sixty-one-year-old Leonardo. Leonardo had been invited to work in Rome by Giuliano de' Medici, who was now the head of the Florentine Medici family. This was one of the most important and powerful families in Florence and in Italy. Giuliano's brother had been made Pope in March and the two of them were living in Rome. Francesco Melzi, Salai and two or three others went with Leonardo from Milan.

Giuliano did everything possible to make Leonardo comfortable in Rome. Although he was a very rich and powerful man, it was said that he treated Leonardo 'more like a brother than a friend'. He gave him rooms in a house called the Belvedere, which sat on a hill on the edge of the city and on one side looked north over the flat valley of the River Tiber and the hills around. On the south side there was a walled garden with a famous collection of beautiful old sculptures, with **fountains** and plants too. There were big gardens on the west as well, so it was almost like living in the country. The Belvedere was near the Pope's official house and the large church of St Peter's.

> The Pope still lives in the same house as the Popes in Leonardo's time. You can visit parts of this and see paintings and sculptures by famous artists, but there is only one painting there by Leonardo. Nobody knew about the painting until 1803. It entered the Pope's collection around 1857.

On 1 December 1513, a list was made of 'things to be done at the Belvedere in the rooms of Leonardo da Vinci.' These included making a window bigger, and bringing in four wooden dining-tables, eight seats without backs and three long seats, and a table on which to make paints. Leonardo probably asked for all these things, perhaps for his assistants and pupils. So we find Leonardo in the Belvedere a few months later noting that he had finished some geometrical sums 'in the room where I study, given to me by Giuliano.'

---

fountain /ˈfaʊntən/ (n) water that is made to climb and then fall through the air, often into a big bowl

The north side of the Belvedere in the early sixteenth century. The Belvedere is in the middle; the Pope's house is on the far left, connected to the Belvedere by a long wall.

We know little about Leonardo's work in Rome, but we do know that he was working on ideas connected with metal mirrors. Giuliano was perhaps interested in these for making heat and fire for military purposes. There was a German metal worker called Giovanni working for Leonardo on these mirrors. But their relationship was not good and Leonardo discovered that Giovanni was making things for other people instead of doing the work for Leonardo and Giuliano de' Medici.

Leonardo made several trips for or with Giuliano. He visited the port of Civitavecchia on the coast north of Rome. He went to Parma, maybe giving advice to Giuliano on castles and military matters. He also, it seems, went to Bologna with the Pope during the autumn of 1515. The Pope was there for an official meeting with the new French king, François I. It was perhaps at this time that Leonardo thought of some ideas to improve the Medici family's house in Florence. This included a big **stable** like the one we will look at in the next chapter.

● Leonardo in France

In March 1516, Giuliano de' Medici died. Six months later, Leonardo was on his way to France to the court of King François I in Amboise on the River Loire. Leonardo was made very welcome in Amboise. He was given the house at Clos Lucé on the edge of Amboise, very close to the king's castle. Leonardo was, it

stable /ˈsteɪbəl/ (n) a building for horses to live in

seems, happy in France, and we know that Francesco Melzi was there to help him and that Salai was with him for some of the time.

Leonardo was also given lots of money and interesting work to do, but not more work than he wanted. For example, from late 1517 until the beginning of 1518 he was in Romorantin. Here François I wanted Leonardo to build him an enormous new house or castle. The idea was to connect it to the River Loire and the River Sâone with canals. Leonardo also had ideas for the gardens, including formal gardens with fountains. One plan was for a big area of water where on special occasions there would be theatrical fights with boats.

Parties were important at court and in June 1518 Leonardo entertained the king at his own house. There was a big tent built next to the house, like an outside room. It had a roof of blue cloth with gold stars on it, like the real sky, as well as the main stars and the sun on one side and the moon on the other. The support posts for the roof were completely covered with green branches and leaves. Remember the room with the trees that Leonardo painted in Milan? Leonardo wanted this tent to give the same feeling that you were outside in a beautiful garden with the night sky above you. In this tent was a platform with a table for the king and other royal guests. Someone at the time said that there were about 400 lamps with flames, and it was so bright '... that it seemed the night was chased away.' In a time before electric or gas lights, this was quite a wonderful and unusual sight.

We can see from all these examples how successful Leonardo was and how people in government wanted him to work for them. They wanted him to make art and sculptures for them; they were interested in his practical ideas for machines, as well as enjoying his skill in inventing clever and beautiful decorations for plays and parties.

Isabella d'Este tried to get a painting from Leonardo for four or five years – this shows how much she wanted a piece of his work. But she was always careful in her letters not to annoy him. She was a very powerful woman, so this shows how much she valued his art. Giuliano de' Medici did his best to make Leonardo's life pleasant and easy. He gave Leonardo the time and space to think and work instead of demanding things from him.

5.1 Were you right?

Look at your notes in Activity 4.4. Then write the missing words in the sentences below.

When Leonardo was in Milan, he invented 'Heaven' for a [1]................................ at

wedding celebrations, and he planned the [2]................................ for soldiers to wear

at a theatrical event. He also made a big clay [3]................................ of a horse for a

[4]................................ sculpture that was never made. In Mantua, he did

[5]................................ of Isabella d'Este. The Florentines wanted Leonardo to

[6]................................ his painting of *The Battle of Anghiari*, but he preferred to work

for the French king in [7]................................ . Then he worked in Rome before moving

to [8]................................ . There he had lots of ideas connected with

[9]................................, like canals and fountains, and had a [10]................................

for the king at his house.

5.2 What more did you learn?

Decide whether these statements about Leonardo are true (✓) or false (✗).

1 He had a lot of different opportunities because he worked
  for rich employers. ☐

2 He always worked alone. ☐

3 He was only interested in making small sculptures. ☐

4 Many of his employers gave him time and space for his studies. ☐

5 Important people wanted to have paintings by him. ☐

6 He finished everything he started. ☐

7 He did everything that he was asked to do. ☐

8 His employers realised that he had different skills. ☐

.3 Language in use

**Look at the sentence in the box.
Show where in each sentence (↑) the
words below it should go.**

> It was called *Il Paradiso*,
> **which** means 'Heaven'.

1 In those days plays were only for the richest people in a city.

↑

, which were performed privately,

2 Leonardo was asked to make an enormous sculpture of a horse.

, who loved horses,

3 He admired Mariolo's horse.

, which had a beautiful neck

4 French soldiers shot at his clay model.

, which completely destroyed it

5 Isabella d'Este sent a messenger to Leonardo.

, who wanted a painting,

6 Leonardo was called to Milan by Charles d'Amboise and the French king.

, whose work they admired,

5.4 What's next?

1 Discuss each of the pictures in Chapter 5 that show Leonardo's ideas and work.

   a What does each picture show?

   b What does it add to our understanding of Leonardo's skills?

2 Discuss how Leonardo's interest in the first of each of these could help with his
work on the second.

   a geometry   buildings

   b horses   stables

   c the movement of water   canals

   d detail   town surveys

Engineer and Architect

Leonardo was trying to sell himself to a powerful man who was interested in protecting his country with castles and soldiers.

In about 1483, Leonardo wrote a letter to Ludovico Sforza in Milan telling him what he could do and therefore why Ludovico should employ him. He said:
I have seen and thought about the works of people who are supposed to be best at making war machines. I will show my ideas and secrets to you and will make what you want.

He then listed some of his ideas for military equipment: light but strong moveable bridges; ways to destroy the enemy's bridges; ladders and bridges for military camps, and ways to stop water filling holes that had been dug; ways of destroying a castle without using big guns; moveable guns that would shoot large numbers of stones; secret ways underneath the ground, even under rivers; covered vehicles that could pass safely among enemy soldiers; unusual big and small guns; machines for throwing stones, and ships that were safe from attack by guns at sea.

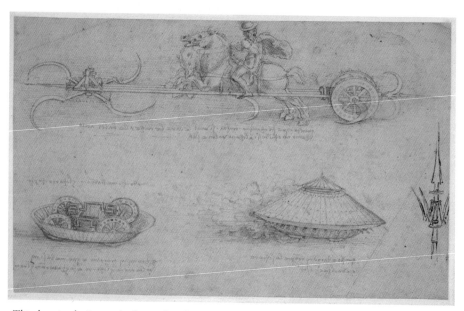

This drawing by Leonardo shows ideas for war machines. The problem with the one at the top is that, as Leonardo said, 'it is as dangerous for your friends as for your enemies!'

He continued that in times of peace he was an architect and good at controlling the movement of water, and he could sculpt and paint. We might be surprised that Leonardo put painting last on the list since it was the thing he was best known for in the 1480s. But Leonardo was trying to sell himself to a powerful man who was interested in protecting his country with castles and soldiers. A man like this wanted military machines that his enemies did not have and clever ways to win wars. It was also quite normal at this time for architects and engineers to train first as painters or sculptors. We can see this too from the list of Ludovico's top engineers in the 1490s:

Bramante, engineer and painter, Giovanni Battagio, engineer and builder, Gian Giacomo Dolcebuono, engineer and sculptor, Leonardo da Vinci, engineer and painter.

All of them also worked as architects.

Leonardo the architect

When Leonardo wrote to Ludovico about his abilities as an architect, we do not know if he had already planned or built anything. We do know, though, that in 1487 he worked on the main church in Milan. This was a big stone building that had been started in 1386. By the middle of the 1480s it was built up to the roof, but one part of the roof needed to be very wide and high and nobody was sure how to do it. Leonardo was paid for six months to work on a wooden model for this with a man who worked in wood. Leonardo had to think about what shape to make the roof and how to make the stones fit together and stay up. So it needed very practical ideas and the skills of an engineer. At the same time this roof needed to be beautiful. Several other architects were asked for solutions, and Leonardo did not win this competition, but in 1490 he was asked to give advice on the main church in Pavia – a large town that was under the control of the Sforza family.

Geometry and mathematics were at the centre of Leonardo's ideas about architecture. He believed that each part of a building had a correct place, so there was a perfect relationship between the smallest and the largest parts. These ideas were connected with the style of architecture that Leonardo liked. This was the style that had been used by the Romans 1,500 years earlier and which became very fashionable again in the fifteenth century. It became a new style instead of appearing old.

Leonardo noted in his writings a couple of times that an architect friend in Milan had a copy of a famous Roman book on architecture – the style that Leonardo and others were very enthusiastic about. During his years in Milan, Leonardo wanted to learn all about architecture and its rules.

● Cities

Leonardo was interested in how people live and how to make their daily lives pleasant. So he made plans for the organisation of cities. Again, he thought about this in very practical ways. Leonardo wanted to destroy poor and nasty houses and to build whole new areas for people to live in. People thought that crowded conditions, especially bad air, spread disease. Fear of this was common, especially as Leonardo and others remembered great sickness and many deaths in Milan in 1484–85. Leonardo suggested that good houses should be built next to wide streets and near a convenient market square with shops round it. In his description and drawings there are streets running on different levels – roads or waterways underneath the ground would be used to take dirt and rubbish out of the city. The purpose was to make the whole city healthy and attractive to live in. Such cities were, he believed, good for the economy because people would come to shop in well organised and beautiful cities, as well as liking to live there.

● Ideas about buildings

Leonardo also thought carefully about single buildings and the best way to plan and build them. For example, he had ideas for the best kind of stable for horses. Horses were important for carrying people around, but the rich also used them for hunting, races, games and war. In one plan for Giuliano de' Medici in Florence, Leonardo recorded that there would be space for 128 horses. We know, of course, that Leonardo himself loved horses. For Leonardo a stable had to work really well and be comfortable for the horses, but it also had to be beautiful. You can see in the drawing above how he chose the new, fashionable

Leonardo's drawing of a perfect stable for horses

style of architecture. The idea here is to keep the horses' food on the floor above the one where the horses live. This keeps the food dry in the middle of the room and there are big windows for light and air. There are holes in the floor so food could easily be dropped down to the horses below. Downstairs, the horses lived along each side of the room. The floor goes down slightly into the centre from the sides. There are some holes in this central part which connect with long holes under the floor. These run the whole length of the building, for easy cleaning of all the waste from the horses.

You can see from Leonardo's city drawing on page 54 that he thought about houses in connection with streets and canals, and each building in connection with other buildings. So he thought about how buildings fitted with other things, including their physical situation. One example was the country house of Agnolo Tovaglia. Agnolo was a rich Florentine businessman and in the summer of 1500 Leonardo went to the hills south of Florence to draw this house. The drawing was sent to Francesco Gonzaga, who governed Mantua, because he had once stayed with Agnolo in the house. He had liked the house so much that he wanted to build one like it for himself. Agnolo wrote to Francesco that Leonardo sent his good wishes to Francesco and his wife Isabella d'Este. Leonardo had said, though, that if Francesco did build a similar building, he would not be able to make it perfect without bringing there the countryside that was around Agnolo's house!

If you cannot move the countryside, you can change the land around a house with gardens. When Leonardo was in Milan, Charles d'Amboise asked him to make plans for a summer house in the country for him just outside the walls of the city. He wanted the house to have big rooms and to open out towards beautiful gardens. Leonardo's notes about ideas for the gardens included plans for a clear stream in which there were clean plants for fish to eat and hide in. There were places filled with birds that sing. There was the lovely smell of flowers. A little canal would run between dining tables and here you could keep the wine cool. Water would power a machine to make the air cool on hot days, as well as fountains and even musical instruments.

The use of water for power was not new; for example, it was used to run machines that prepared and broke seeds for making bread. But Leonardo was very interested in it and wanted to make even more use of water power to run machines. Again, we find Leonardo bringing his different interests together – here machines, nature and landscape.

● Controlling the movement of water

People also used water for moving things around. It was easier to carry heavy things or large quantities on boats instead of using horses on muddy and rocky roads. So engineers dug canals to improve the use of rivers and water. Canals meant that you could travel where there was no river, or where a river was not deep enough for boats. Leonardo examined and studied a lot of rivers and canals. There was great skill in knowing how to dig canals or to control large quantities of water that might appear suddenly after heavy rain. So in 1483 when Leonardo included controlling the movement of water as one of his skills, this was a very important activity. We have already seen how his studies show a knowledge and understanding of the energy and force of water. This included how rivers moved earth and stones and could even change direction as these attacked their edges. The drawing of water in Chapter 2, where the water falls from above, shows it coming out of a man-made hole, showing how water can be made even more powerful if it is controlled. The other two drawings of water in Chapter 2 show water meeting something and changing direction. You can imagine how Leonardo used that idea for the building of a bridge where parts of it were in a river and always being hit by water.

Early in 1494, Leonardo had the chance to increase his knowledge of how canals worked and how the control of water was useful for farming. At this time he was staying to the east of Milan, near a small town called Vigevano. This was the town where Ludovico Sforza had been born. Ludovico owned farms all round there and in the 1480s he had had a lot of work done to improve the land, to grow more food. Many canals had been dug to stop the land being wet all the time. Water on other parts of the land was kept and controlled because rice was grown there. Leonardo looked at these canals and ways that water was stopped or made to run slower or faster.

Rivers and canals were also important in times of war to move things around and for defence, because they could be used like a fence against an enemy. If you look at the map of Imola on page 60, you can see how water around the outside of it helped to protect the town from attack. At the beginning of 1500 Leonardo went to Venice for a short time. While he was there he went on a trip north east along the coast into the area called Friuli, which was under the control of the Venetians. He was asked to find ways to defend the River Isonzo and its towns against attack from Turkish soldiers coming from the east. Leonardo wrote a report on the situation for the government in Venice. He decided that the river's speed and power meant that it needed to be controlled if defences were built on the river itself. The government probably took his advice and Leonardo gave them a plan of what to make.

In his report Leonardo said that he had looked at the river and he had also talked to farmers there because they knew about local conditions. This reminds us of how much Leonardo valued experience – his own and the experience of other people. It also tells us that people were happy to talk to him. Of course Leonardo had also spent part of his childhood in the country, so he understood farmers' lives and the subjects they talked about.

● Leonardo the military engineer: in Romagna with Cesare Borgia

Leonardo probably learnt a lot about military architecture when he worked for Ludovico Sforza, and he used this knowledge in the summer of 1502 when he worked for Cesare Borgia, giving advice on castles and other matters.

Cesare was the son of Pope Alexander VI and in charge of the Pope's army, although he was only about twenty-seven. He was married to a cousin of King Louis XII of France and had helped the French army take Milan in 1499. For the next couple of years, French soldiers had helped his army as Cesare took control of a large part of central Italy – the area called Romagna. Florence was very worried about all of this because Cesare was taking towns and countryside on the border of Florentine land. In 1501 the Florentines decided to pay Cesare a large amount of money to work for them. It was really a gift that they had to give him to stop him attacking Florence. But then the situation became more frightening a year later when the town of Arezzo, which was under Florentine control, decided to accept Cesare's protection instead of Florence's. Florentine ambassadors, including Niccolo Macchiavelli, went to see Cesare in Urbino at the end of June. Cesare said that he knew the Florentines did not like him and 'if you will not have me as your friend you will know me as your enemy.' Machiavelli wrote back to Florence that 'there is no job so large that it does not seem small to Cesare' and that he was 'popular with his soldiers and he has collected the best men in Italy.' So the Florentines needed to stay friendly with him.

Leonardo entered Cesare's service in Urbino, in June 1502. Leonardo had, perhaps, already met him when the French took Milan, because Cesare was with them. Three years later Cesare was not officially at war with Florence, so the Florentine Leonardo was not going to work for the enemy. But the situation was difficult and we have seen that the Florentines were worried. Was Leonardo a kind of spy for the Florentines? Cesare did not, it seems, think this was a possibility because he asked Leonardo to make surveys of the areas and cities that Cesare now controlled, including military castles. In Leonardo's passport, dated 18 August 1502, Cesare states that free movement everywhere under his rule should be given to:

my most excellent and my preferred Architect and General Engineer Leonardo da Vinci, who will survey the places and castles of my land at my request. He should be given all the help that he needs.

Leonardo started his travels from Urbino, where he surveyed the city's walls. He travelled quickly from place to place, recording things in a small notebook. He also drew or noted down things that interested him which sometimes had no connection with his job. In Urbino, for example, he drew a bird house, and some architectural details of the very famous enormous main house in the town. He travelled from Urbino to Pesaro, and then up the eastern coast of Italy to Rimini, where he noted the musical sounds that came from a fountain as a

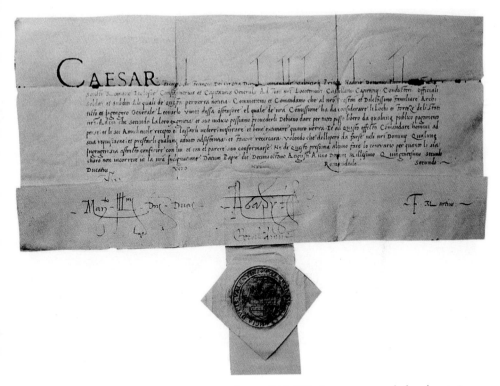

Leonardo's passport from Cesare Borgia, 18 August 1502. This document was only found again in 1792. It comes from the Melzi family collection in Vaprio d'Adda. It is written in Latin and you can see Cesare Borgia's name, 'Caesar', in capital letters at the beginning. He takes advantage of the fact that his name in Latin means 'head of the army'.

result of water falling in different ways. He drew a boat on the sea there and was interested in how the force of the wind filled its sail and moved the boat forward. As he travelled, he was interested in life in the countryside. He noted how the men looking after the sheep in the area of Cesena communicated with each other. They blew instruments into a hole in the side of a hill and this made the sound louder and go farther. He also made a drawing of the method that farmers used to hang up bunches of ripe fruit. On the coast at Cesenatico, he measured the port and drew a view from above of the area around. Leonardo arrived in Imola on 10 September, and stayed there for between one and three months.

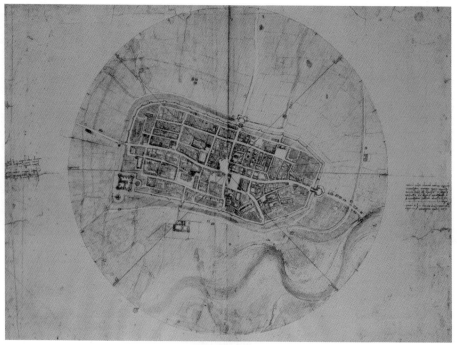

Leonardo's map of Imola, 1502

While he was in Imola Leonardo surveyed the city very carefully and drew a complete map of it, which you can see above. It shows us the city and an area around it. The city's streets and buildings are marked in detail within the walls, then fields and roads are drawn around the city, and the curves of the river to the south. Leonardo used different colours for buildings, open spaces in the town, fields outside the walls of the town, and waterways. On the left and right of the drawing of the town, Leonardo wrote down the distance and direction to other towns and cities. So he placed Imola in relationship to a larger area. This is the kind of information that was useful to a soldier. It also reminds us that Leonardo always connected the small to the large in the world.

Maps in Leonardo's time were made by taking exact measurements of things on the ground and using geometry to place buildings and other things. This took time and had to be done with care. There were no electronic machines to help or to do the sums. Everything was drawn by hand as well.

● Advising the Florentines on military matters

Leonardo's experiences with Cesare Borgia probably added to his practical knowledge of military architecture. He was able to measure, draw and improve castles. We can see him making use of this skill in June 1503. Since the 1490s, the Florentines had tried with their army to take control of the city of Pisa on the west coast of Italy. On 19 June 1503 they took a little castle called La Verruca and Leonardo advised on ways of improving its defences.

As part of the Florentine fight against the Pisans, Leonardo gave advice on a much larger and more difficult plan. This was to cut a canal and make the River Arno run south of Pisa instead of through it. The Florentines intended to stop the Pisans bringing food into their city and sending soldiers out. You can see in the picture below what was planned.

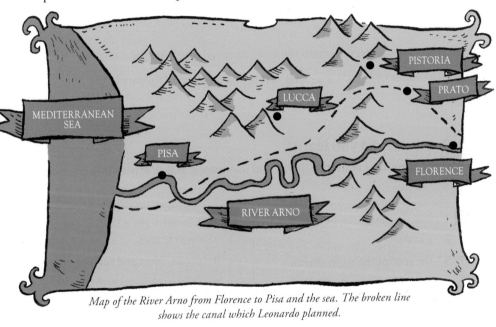

Map of the River Arno from Florence to Pisa and the sea. The broken line shows the canal which Leonardo planned.

Leonardo had been very interested in the idea of a canal for part of the River Arno for some time; a straight, deep canal would make it easier for boats to go from Florence to the sea because the river had lots of curves and shallow parts. The water in the canal could also be controlled, so there would not be problems in the summer when the River Arno was often low or dry. Work on the plan to stop the river entering Pisa did start a year later, but Leonardo was not employed on this and his plans were not followed completely. After two months the whole plan was given up – it had been an expensive disaster.

6.1 Were you right?

Think back to your discussions for Activity 5.4. Then read the sentences. Only one of them is true. Which one? Correct the others by crossing out words and writing the right words.

1 It was unusual for architects and engineers to be trained artists. ....

2 Leonardo disliked the old Roman style of architecture. ....

3 Rich people only used horses for travelling. ....

4 It was easier to move heavy things on canals than by road. ....

5 Leonardo had little understanding of farmers' lives. ....

6 Maps of surrounding areas were less useful to soldiers than town maps.

   ....

7 The Pisans wanted to make the River Arno run south of Pisa. ....

8 The Florentines built the canal that Leonardo planned for part of the Arno.

   ....

6.2 What more did you learn?

Match Leonardo's activities, ideas and inventions in Box A with information in Box B.

A		**B**	
1	war machines	a	a healthy place to live, with open spaces
2	a stable	b	plants, birds and running water
3	the roof of the main church in Milan	c	skills in military architecture
4	a report on the defence of the River Isonzo	d	dangerous to your enemies, but sometimes also to your friends
5	surveys of city walls	e	high, wide and beautiful
6	a new city	f	the experiences of local farmers
7	plans for gardens	g	a warm, dry place
8	advice on the defence of a castle	h	carefully measured and hand-drawn

6.3 Language in use

Look at the sentences in the box. Then rewrite the sentences below using passive verb forms.

> He **should be given** all the help that he needs.
>
> Food **could** easily **be dropped** down to the horses below.

1 People must give Leonardo freedom of movement

Leonardo *must be given freedom of movement* .

2 They had to find ways of moving under rivers.

Ways ....

3 Rich people might use artists as architects.

Artists ....

4 We ought to employ Leonardo for the church roof.

Leonardo ....

5 People from other towns would visit attractive cities.

Attractive cities ....

6 Water could power machines for cooling the air.

Machines ....

6.4 What's next?

Read the words in *italics* below the title of Chapter 6, and look at the pictures in the chapter.

Discuss why Leonardo is still so famous today, and make notes below.

Notes

Inventions, Games and Success

'I cannot believe a man has ever been born who knew as much as Leonardo, and not only about sculpture, painting and architecture.'

Leonardo was a great thinker and inventor; he also liked to have fun and to stretch his mind with word and number games. His skill was to see something in nature and then think how to use that for solving human problems. A lot of his ideas probably stayed on paper, and other people only matched some of his inventions much later. Leonardo's studies helped him to make games and machines for people's fun and pleasure. But he had ideas for making useful machines too – machines that could work harder than humans or animals, or that could do things that humans could not do.

● Birds and flying machines

If you remember, Leonardo said that his first memory as a child was of a bird. There is also a story that he bought birds that had been caught and freed them. He continued to love birds and, most importantly, to watch how they flew and then to record what he saw in notes and drawings. For example, he drew a lot of little pictures of a bird flying, and how the bird used the air. Leonardo quickly caught the shapes of the bird's wings, or the way that one wing was lifted higher, or how it used its tail to hold itself as it wanted in the air. Next to each drawing he made notes. He did this in a whole book that he wrote and drew in April 1505 about birds flying. All this shows how important seeing, looking and understanding were to him.

Leonardo connected his interest in birds with his interest in machines. He began to think about how a person might fly. He noted that:

The beating of its wings against the air can support a heavy bird in the thin air closer to the sun [and] from this man can learn, with large wings tied to him ... how to lift himself.

He watched how birds flew and he also made careful drawings of the bones of birds' wings. His first ideas were to make a machine with wings that went up and down. He decided, though, that a bird's wings let air through, so were not the best idea for a man's wings. You can see from the drawing opposite that he chose a different model – the wing of a **bat**. So his wings for a man were made of cloth stretched between very light and thin pieces of wood. Everything was tied together with leather. He also used pieces of curved metal, kept bent under force. But a lot of power is needed to make wings that beat up and down; in the

---

bat /bæt/ (n) a small animal like a mouse with wings that flies around at night

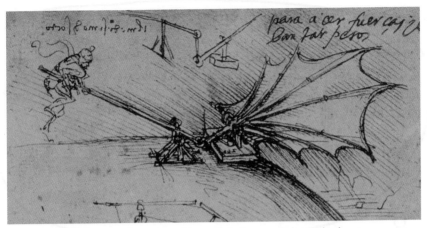

Leonardo's drawing of a wing machine and the force needed to make the wing move

drawing, the man is moving the wing with the power of a **lever**. This is much more than the normal strength of a man. But even with a machine to drive levers, it is not possible, without electricity, for a man to make a wing like this work in the air for very long. So Leonardo thought of fixed wings. This means, though, that you could only fly from a high point to a lower one.

We are not sure if Leonardo made any of these machines full-size. To test flight, he wrote:

The machine should be tried over a lake. You should carry a leather bag full of air tied to your waist, so if you fall in the water you will be safe.

We do not know if Leonardo or any of his assistants ever did try this!

This kind of fixed wing machine was not made well until 1920. In the late twentieth century, a full-size copy of one of Leonardo's flying machines with fixed wings was made for a TV programme. The machine flew farther than the first flight by the American Wright brothers' aeroplane in 1903! This was not very far, maybe, but it shows how nobody came close to matching Leonardo's ideas until almost five hundred years after his death. Leonardo also had the idea of a kind of pointed cloth tent about seven metres high, underneath which a man hung, connected to it by leather belts and ties. The cloth was fixed to pieces of wood and was open at the bottom. If the man then jumped off a high place or building, the cloth filled with air and supported him so he fell gently. We now call this a **parachute**. The first parachutes were made in the late 1700s, although they did not follow Leonardo's model.

lever /ˈliːvə/ (n) a stick that you push down at one end to help lift a heavy weight at the other end
parachute /ˈpærəʃuːt/ (n) a piece of equipment to bring you safely down to the ground that is fixed to the back of people who jump out of planes

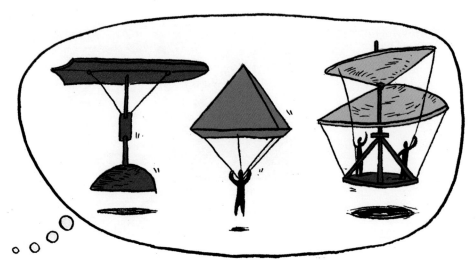

*Leonardo's ideas for a flying machine with a fixed wing, a parachute and a **helicopter**.*
The first helicopter to get off the ground was built in France in 1907 by Paul Cornu,
but the first real flight was made in 1924 by the Frenchman Etienne Oehmichen.

● Machines for moving through and under water

Leonardo was interested in movement through air, but he was also interested in movement through water. We saw in Chapter 2 how he connected the shapes of water with the shapes of hair and knots, or the form of the veins in the body with the shapes of trees or the movement of water in rivers. He also compared the movements of birds through the air and fish through water. He thought of making a boat that was moved by wheels at the sides that had boards on them. Men made the wheels move by stepping on levers; as the wheels turned, the boards went into the water and pushed the boat forwards.

He also thought of ways that would allow a person to stay and even walk around under water. Some ideas, he said, he would not describe because they would help enemy attacks on ships at sea. But he did describe a kind of head covering to wear under the water with two breathing tubes going up to a bell-shaped machine that sat on the surface of the water. One tube let air in and the other let it out. Equipment like this does in fact work in shallow water. Leonardo had an idea too for a coat that had a leather bag to hold air so you could stay under water for some time. Clothes and machines for diving under water were made and used from the sixteenth century, but they were not very safe or easy to use. A good way to control the movement of air through breathing tubes was only found in 1943.

helicopter /ˈhelɪkɒptə/ (n) an aeroplane that flies by turning a narrow wing around flat in the air very fast

● Leonardo's games

Leonardo loved jokes in words and pictures. He liked jokes that played with words and ideas. For example: 'Many people will be busy taking away from a thing that will get bigger as it gets less.' What is it? Answer: 'A hole in the ground.' 'What is a body that grows when the head is taken from it, and gets smaller when the head is put back?' Answer: 'A pillow.' 'Who walks on top of trees?' Answer: 'A man wearing shoes made of wood.'

One of Leonardo's many picture and word plays – 'leonardesco'

His picture jokes also show him playing around with ideas. On one sheet of paper Leonardo put together 154 drawings of pictures of things whose names, when read or spoken, can mean, or sound like, something else. For example in the drawing above you can see that he drew a **lion** (*leone* in Italian) in a fire (*ardere* means 'to burn' in Italian) next to a table (*desco* in Italian); all this adds up to *leonardesco*, which is the adjective for the name Leonardo. Remember that Leonardo wrote from right to left – and that is true of the pictures here as well as the words!

Leonardo also liked to play with numbers, which shows his mathematical skill as well as his taste for games. Here is an example:

Put equal numbers of beans in each hand.
Move four beans from your right hand to your left hand.
Throw away the rest of the beans in your right hand.
Throw away the same number of beans from your left hand.
Pick up and add five beans to your left hand.
At the end you will always have thirteen beans in your left hand.

◆

His practical scientific interests and abilities also helped Leonardo in his life at court. He was asked to make all sorts of things to amuse people. He invented a machine that played bells. He had an idea for a clock run by water to help you to wake up. When it reached the right time, the feet of the person sleeping were pulled up into the air. He was a chemist because he could turn white wine into red. He also had clever ideas for hidden fountains in gardens that shot water into the air when you stepped or sat on something. People at court lived a very formal life and so they enjoyed these kinds of jokes in places like gardens where they relaxed.

Leonardo knew how to make machines that moved and he used this knowledge for special occasions. He probably made a machine in the shape of a lion that was used by Florentines in Lyons, France, in July 1515 to celebrate the arrival of the new French king, François I. They chose a lion because it was a symbol of Florence. The lion walked forward a few steps, which was a little frightening, but then its chest opened to show lots of *fleurs-de-lys*, a flower that was symbolic of both Florence and France. So the whole thing was a friendly joke.

● Leonardo's ideas – looking at and thinking about the world

It has been suggested that Leonardo's character stopped him from finishing anything; because he was interested in so many things, he always wanted to discover and know everything. A sign of this is that Leonardo wrote and drew different things on the same sheet of paper or in the same book, even if he started by intending to think about only one subject. In one collection of notes, he wrote:

Reader, do not be surprised or laugh at me if here I jump around from subject to subject.

Leonardo did not go to university and felt the need to defend himself against people who might criticise his ideas because of this. He wrote that readers of books often know only other people's thoughts instead of having their own:

Experience is the teacher of all who have written well, and so – as it is my

lion /ˈlaɪən/ (n) a very large yellow wild cat that usually lives in Africa and Asia *teacher – I will use it and talk about it all the time.*

In fact, though, Leonardo read books of all kinds, probably some in Latin but more in Italian. Around 1495 he listed about forty books that he owned – this was quite a lot for that time. He also used libraries and the collections of people he knew.

● Success and rewards

It perhaps suited Leonardo to work for a court instead of painting pictures or planning buildings for lots of different people. But when he worked for Ludovico Sforza he was not always paid regularly. There are letters from him to Ludovico saying that his situation was difficult and that he had to do work for others to have enough money for himself and his assistants to live. He was always careful, though, to make this sound like the fault of Sforza's officials and not Sforza himself. In one letter he wrote:

If you were told that I had money, this was not true. I had to feed six men for fifty-six months and have had fifty ducats from your officials.

This was not enough money for all his costs.

He was not always paid on time by Ludovico Sforza, but he was rewarded by him. On 26 April 1499 Ludovico Sforza recorded the gift to Leonardo, 'most famous Florentine painter', of a large garden just outside the walls of Milan. It was about 200 metres by 50 metres in size. Leonardo thought its value was about 1,931 ducats. This gift was in recognition of Leonardo's 'wonderful and clever works' and his 'most unusual abilities'. Ludovico said that Leonardo was free to build there if he wanted to, or to use it as a garden. It was not far from Santa Maria delle Grazie – the monastery where Leonardo painted *The Last Supper*; it was also near the house of Galeazzo Sanseverino. It was perhaps in Galeazzo's stables there that Leonardo had looked at Galeazzo's handsome horses. Leonardo lost this garden when the French took Milan, but it was given back to him by the French in April 1507. This is the garden that Leonardo separated into two parts when he died. Salai had already built a house there, which Leonardo gave to him; the other half Leonardo gave to a servant called Battista de Vilanis. When Leonardo was working for the French in Milan, he was paid very well. Charles d'Amboise probably gave him gifts too. King Louis XII also allowed him to receive the taxes paid by the users of a canal in Milan.

When Leonardo moved to France, the French paid him even more money. By 1517 he was receiving 1,000 écus a year and he was given the title 'First Painter and Engineer and Architect of the king'. The French government also paid Francesco Melzi and Salai, who were living with and working for Leonardo. One clear sign of François' pleasure was the gift of the house at Clos Lucé, and the fact that it was close to François' own house in Amboise. You can see a picture of it below. It had been built only about twenty years before Leonardo received it.

Leonardo's house at Clos Lucé on the edge of Amboise

From all this we know that François I had a very good opinion of Leonardo and wanted to keep him in France. In the 1540s, twenty years after Leonardo had died, François told Benvenuto Cellini, another Florentine artist who came to work for him in France, that 'I cannot believe a man has ever been born who knew as much as Leonardo, and not only about sculpture, painting and architecture. He was also a very great thinker.' François also liked Leonardo; Cellini said that the king 'was completely crazy about Leonardo's abilities and took such pleasure in hearing him talk that there were few days in the year when he was separated from him.'

● Leonardo, 'Renaissance Man'

We can see that Leonardo was admired and rewarded by those who valued all his abilities as an artist, engineer and thinker. He has excited interest from the time when he was alive until today. The quality of his paintings, studies and inventions means that many people today call Leonardo a 'Renaissance Man'. They mean that he had such great artistic and scientific abilities that he brought together in one person much knowledge and many different kinds of ideas. His ideas and interests stretched from the useful to the beautiful.

Leonardo's work has also received unwelcome attention, though. In 1962 a man threw a bottle of ink at a very large drawing by Leonardo of *The Virgin and Child with St Anne*, in London's National Gallery. Fortunately the bottle did not break, and after that a sheet of glass was put up to protect it. But in 1987 a man took out a gun and shot at the picture. At that time the drawing was thought to have a value of more than $35 million, and the man knew that it would be a big news story. The force of the bullet meant that glass damaged the picture. There were about sixty very small pieces of paper to fit together and it took more than a year to repair it. In the end only about one square centimetre of the drawing was lost.

Leonardo's paintings, his drawings and his ideas continue to give people pleasure and to make them think. Although he only managed to paint a small number of paintings, he is still one of the most famous painters in the world. Many people even want to see works that he did not finish, like the painting of *The Adoration of the Magi* in the Uffizi Gallery in Florence, which Leonardo began in that city in March 1481.

Leonardo had just turned sixty-seven when he died, but he had succeeded in doing many things during his life. In his own words: 'Life, if it is well spent, is long.' One can say too that Leonardo lives today in his art and his inventions.

1 **Work in small groups. Discuss Leonardo's words, and the questions below them, and then make notes on either A or B.**

A *Experience is the teacher of all who have written well.*

What else might a writer (or artist) use?

How important do *you* think personal experience is when producing literature or art? Why?

Is experience always possible?

B *Although clever humans make different inventions, they can never find any inventions more beautiful, better matched to their purpose or clearer than nature's.*

What are the cleverest inventions that humans have made, in your opinion?

What do you think are nature's greatest 'inventions'?

Has nature made any 'mistakes'?

Do you agree with Leonardo's statement?

Notes

2 **Find another group that has made notes on the same subject. Discuss Leonardo's words with them. Do you all agree?**

Choose a painting by Leonardo from this book that you really like. What does it show? Why do you think it is generally admired? Why do you like it? Write about the painting below.

1 Work in small groups. Choose an invention by Leonardo – either from this book or by searching on the Internet. Some are shown below. Find out more about the invention, using libraries and the Internet, and make notes in your notebooks.

2 **Make a presentation on the invention you have chosen to the other groups.**

Explain:
- what it is
- what it is for
- what it is made of
- how big it is
- how easy or difficult it would be to make
- how it is connected to inventions since that time
- why it was or was not made at the time

As you listen to the other presentations, complete the table below. Give each invention marks out of ten.

Invention	Usefulness	Clever idea	Beauty

3 **Imagine that you live in Leonardo's time and are very rich and powerful.**

A Agree as a class which of the inventions in the table above you would like Leonardo to make for you and why. How would you use it?

B What would you need to give Leonardo to help him complete his job? Make a list of things he would need.

4 **Imagine that Leonardo has now made the invention for you and has moved to France. Write to him explaining how you have used it, how successful it has been and whether it could be improved.**